Harold Innis

CRITICAL MEDIA STUDIES
INSTITUTIONS, POLITICS, AND CULTURE

Series Editor
Andrew Calabrese, University of Colorado

Advisory Board

Patricia Aufderheide,
American University
Jean-Claude Burgelman,
Free University of Brussels
Simone Chambers,
University of Toronto
Nicholas Garnham,
University of Westminster
Hanno Hardt,
University of Iowa
Gay Hawkins,
The University of New South Wales
Maria Heller,
Eötvös Loránd University
Robert Horwitz,
University of California at San Diego
Douglas Kellner,
University of California at Los Angeles
Gary Marx,
Massachusetts Institute of Technology
Toby Miller,
New York University

Vincent Mosco,
Queen's University
Janice Peck,
University of Colorado
Manjunath Pendakur,
Southern Illinois University
Arvind Rajagopal,
New York University
Kevin Robins,
Goldsmiths College
Saskia Sassen,
University of Chicago
Colin Sparks,
University of Westminster
Slavko Splichal,
University of Ljubljana
Thomas Streeter,
University of Vermont
Liesbet van Zoonen,
University of Amsterdam
Janet Wasko,
University of Oregon

Recent Titles in the Series

Critical Communication Theory: Power, Media, Gender, and Technology, Sue Curry
    Jansen
Digital Disability: The Social Construction of Disability in New Media, Gerard Goggin
    and Christopher Newell
Principles of Publicity and Press Freedom, Slavko Splichal
Internet Governance in Transition: Who Is the Master of This Domain? Daniel J. Paré
Recovering a Public Vision for Public Television, Glenda R. Balas
Reality TV: The Work of Being Watched, Mark Andrejevic
Contesting Media Power: Alternative Media in a Networked World, edited by Nick
    Couldry and James Curran
Herbert Schiller, Richard Maxwell
Harold Innis, Paul Heyer

Forthcoming in the Series

Toward a Political Economy of Culture: Capitalism and Communication in the Twenty-First Century, edited by Andrew Calabrese and Colin Sparks

Public Service Broadcasting in Italy, Cinzia Padovani

Changing Concepts of Time, Harold A. Innis

Many Voices, One World, Seán MacBride

Film Industries and Cultures in Transition, Dina Iordanova

Globalizing Political Communication, Gerald Sussman

The Blame Game: Why Television Is Not Our Fault, Eileen R. Meehan

Mass Communication and Social Thought, edited by John Durham Peters and Peter Simonson

Entertaining the Citizen: When Politics and Popular Culture Converge, Liesbet van Zoonen

Elusive Autonomy: Brazilian Communications Policy, Sergio Euclides de Souza

Harold Innis

Paul Heyer

ROWMAN & LITTLEFIELD PUBLISHERS, INC.
Lanham • Boulder • New York • Toronto • Oxford

ROWMAN & LITTLEFIELD PUBLISHERS, INC.

Published in the United States of America
by Rowman & Littlefield Publishers, Inc.
A wholly owned subsidary of The Rowman & Littlefield Publishing Group, Inc.
4501 Forbes Boulevard, Suite 200, Lanham, Maryland 20706
www.rowmanlittlefield.com

P.O. Box 317, Oxford OX2 9RU, United Kingdom

The photos of Harold Innis on pages xv and 8 appear courtesy of the University of Toronto
Archives.
The photo of Mary Quayle Innis on page 114 is reprinted courtesy of Michael Shaw, Ashley
and Crippen Photography.

British Library Cataloguing in Publication Information Available

Library of Congress Cataloging-in-Publication Data

Heyer, Paul, 1946–
   Harold Innis / Paul Heyer.
      p. cm.— (Critical media studies)
   Includes bibliographical references and index.
   ISBN 0–7425–2483–3 (alk. paper)—ISBN 0–7425–2484–1 (pbk. : alk.
paper)
    1. Innis, Harold Adams, 1894–1952.   2. Mass media
specialists—Canada—Biography.   3. Economists—Canada—Biography.   I.
Title. II. Series.
P92.5.I56H37   2003
330′.092—dc21   2003009123

Printed in the United States of America

∞ ™ The paper used in this publication meets the minimum requirements of American
National Standard for Information Sciences—Permanence of Paper for Printed Library
Materials, ANSI/NISO Z39.48–1992.

To Anne Innis Dagg

Contents

Preface   xi

1 The Road to Political Economy   1

2 From Fur to Fish   11

3 Political Economy Inspires Communication Studies   29

4 The "History of Communications" Project   41

5 Time, Space, and the Oral Tradition   59

6 Monopolies of Knowledge and the Critique of Culture   75

7 An Enduring Legacy   85

Epilogue   101

Appendix A: Harold A. Innis's "History of Communications"
Manuscript   103
   William J. Buxton

Appendix B: The Contributions of Mary Quayle Innis   113
   J. David Black

A Select Bibliography   123

Index   129

About the Author   133

Preface

His name may not be as well known as that of Marshall McLuhan, his University of Toronto colleague and spiritual descendent, but Harold Innis's (1894–1952) influence on contemporary critical media and communication studies has been no less profound. Among media scholars in the United States, Daniel J. Czitrom is certainly not alone when he declares that for the "most radical and elaborate American media theory, one must look to the work of two Canadians, Harold Adams Innis and Marshall McLuhan."[1] James W. Carey sees this patrimony in more asymmetric terms when he declares that, regardless of its difficulties, it is Innis's work, not McLuhan's, "which is the great achievement in communications on this continent."[2]

Despite the increasing recognition Innis is receiving in scholarly circles worldwide, most commentaries on his legacy have been limited to specialist publications—the one biography that exists is brief and barely mentions the communication-related concerns of his later years.[3] Something along the lines of a basic introduction to Innis that could help both students and general readers access his thought has been long overdue.

When the editors at Rowman and Littlefield told me about their *Critical Media Studies Series,* "Masters and Concepts," and asked if I would be interested in contributing a volume on Innis, I felt it was an idea whose time had come and gladly accepted the challenge. In the past, I had written a few things specifically about Innis, although my recent work as a media historian has taken me in other directions. Nevertheless, I keep returning to Innis in order to make better sense of numerous issues pertaining to communication and culture—historically and in terms of today's world—as do many researchers in a variety of disciplines.

To understand Innis's legacy and why it has such contemporary resonance, it will be necessary to chart his intellectual development: from his early research in political economy to his later forays into the then unchartered realm of media and communication studies. Readers will be introduced to some of the formative influences, personal as well as scholarly, that shaped his thought. Most of the book, however, will focus on his later work in critical media studies and communications history. This will entail explaining the key concepts in his intellectual toolkit. My goal is to help readers attain a better grasp of this contribution, both on its own terms and with respect to the relevance it has had for later researchers.

Yet, as with any major thinker, there can be no substitute for reading the primary sources. Unfortunately, Innis's later writings are oftentimes as difficult as they are rich. Students can perhaps gain some solace from the fact that the nature of the difficulty is stylistic rather than conceptual, which places almost everyone on equal footing—there are no interpretive experts when it comes to Innis, and his basic concepts are accessible enough. I will, however, suggest certain strategies for reading or rereading him that might make Innis more approachable—and possibly engaging—for potential readers.

Although this study is not a biography in the strict sense, a certain amount of biographical material can help give the reader a sense of Innis's origins, especially since several of his early life experiences prefigure the later interest in communications. It will be therefore necessary in the first chapter to discuss his odyssey from the farm to the academy and then his subsequent sojourn at the University of Chicago. During the 1920s and 1930s, he worked primarily in political economy and economic history. This phase of his career should not be without interest to students of media and communication, for it is here where Innis begins writing about the importance of transportation and the disparities that exist between urban centers (of empire in his day) and the regional (or colonial) margins that provide them with staple resources—concerns that would ultimately lead him to a critical examination of communications, knowledge, and power on the world stage.

The remaining chapters will focus on Innis the scholar of media and communication. Nevertheless, it must be remembered that this concern emerges only during the last decade of his life, after he had already established an international reputation for his economic studies. No doubt I will be rightly chastised by some Innisophiles for overemphasizing the communications concerns of his later years at the expense of what went before. In defense of this approach, I can only plead that Innis's primary international audience today, including most readers of this book, is more interested in his later work. I will, of course, cite useful commentaries on the early Innis that can be pursued by those whose interest is so inclined.

As will be shown in the remaining chapters, Innis's later work elaborates on three related themes: first, he develops an outline for the study of what is now referred to as communications history or media history, a field for which he remains the definitive cartographer; second, he elaborates several key theoretical concepts for the study of communication and culture, such as medium, time-bias and space-bias, the oral tradition, and the monopoly of knowledge; and third, he suggests how his approach to history and perspective that recent commentators have referred to as "medium theory" can inform a critique of culture and technology in the contemporary world. These contributions have influenced later media researchers, some of whom will be assessed in the concluding chapter. As I hope to show, their work demonstrates that Innis's legacy is not just a formalized system awaiting interpretation, but a resource to be applied as well as studied.

Regardless of how ably or not I carry out my task in the pages that follow, I am sure most will agree that the idea for such a study is timely. Full credit must go to Andrew Calabrese and Brenda Hadenfeldt at Rowman & Littlefield, who deemed a book on Innis essential to their series. From the outset, when they asked if I might be interested in the project, through all the various stages of production, they have been as supportive and congenial an editorial team as an author could have. Jehanne Schweitzer and the production staff at Rowman & Littlefield, as well as Steven Long, who copyedited the manuscript, have been an absolute delight with which to work.

I am also fortunate to have secured the assistance of two colleagues whose Innisian expertise is evident in the two appendices that grace this volume. William J. Buxton discusses the significance and fate of Innis's important but unpublished "History of Communications" manuscript, and J. David Black examines the largely unheralded work of Innis's wife and intellectual partner, Mary Quayle Innis. We wish to thank archivists at both the University of Waterloo and the University of Toronto, especially the latter's Garron Wells and Harold Averill; Mary Cates, daughter of Harold and Mary Innis, for sharing her experience within the Innis family; Michael Shaw, the owner of Ashley and Crippen photography, for the use of Mary Innis's photo; and Lynne Hanna for editorial assistance on appendix B.

Over the years, I have profited greatly from discussions about Innis I have had with Carole Akazawa, Bob Anderson, Bob Babe, Alison Beale, Ted Carpenter, Hart Cohen, David Crowley, Blair Davis, Ron Diebert, Daniel Drache, Virgil Duff, Kathleen Galarneau, Liss Jeffrey, Sut Jhally, Yasmin Jiwani, Rolly Lorimer, Gary McCarron, Bill Melody, Heather Menzies, Florian Morelli, John Durham Peters, Julie Pong, Andrew Preston, Firoozeh Radjei, Gertrude Robinson, Myles Ruggles, Liora Salter, Brian Shoesmith, Collette Snowdon, Don Theall, Gail Valaskakis, Robert Walker, and Ania Zofia. I am also grateful for the enthusiastic support I received throughout the research and writing of this book from members of the department of communication studies at Wilfrid Laurier University, Sylvia Hoang, Iwona Irwin-Zarecka, Herbert Pimlott, Nancy Shaw, James Wong, and Dean of Arts, Robert Campbell.

Finally, special thanks and the dedication must go to Anne Innis Dagg. She graciously offered insights into the life and legacy of her parents and provided invaluable editorial assistance.

NOTES

1. Daniel J. Czitrom, *Media and the American Mind: From Morse to McLuhan* (Chapel Hill: University of North Carolina Press, 1982), 147.

2. James W. Carey, *Communication and Culture: Essays on Media and Society* (Boston: Unwin Hyman, 1989), 142.

3. Donald Grant Creighton, *Harold Adams Innis: Portrait of a Scholar* (1957; reprint, Toronto: University of Toronto Press, 1978).

Harold A. Innis

I have attempted to suggest that Western civilization has been profoundly influenced by communication and that marked changes in communications have had important implications.

—Harold A. Innis

Chapter One

The Road to Political Economy

The economic history of Canada has been dominated by the discrepancy between the centre and the margins of Western civilization.

—Harold A. Innis

He was a child of the soil, not the polis. Born in 1894, the same year as Aldous Huxley and Oliver Wendell Holmes, Harold Innis eventually became one of Canada's most revered scholars. Legend has it that the name on his birth certificate reads "Herald." If so, it would aptly foreshadow both the new directions in political economy his early work would make possible as well as the continually expanding vistas inspired by the communications project that consumed him prior to his premature death from cancer in 1952.

Southwestern Ontario, the land of his birth, is agriculturally rich. The Innis family farm, modest by the standards of the region, was located more than the proverbial stone's throw from large metropolitan areas. Detroit was 120 miles to the west; Cleveland almost the same distance south across Lake Erie; and 90 miles to the east, on the shores of lake Ontario, stood the province's largest city, Toronto, where he would eventually attend university. This possibility, however, seemed unlikely in the earth-clotted years of his early childhood. What was certain was the necessity of making the land yield in the face of the vicissitudes of weather and markets.

His father, William Anson Innis, was a descendant of James Innis, who had fought for the British in the American Revolutionary War and had been granted land in Canada, in the province of New Brunswick, for his service. By the second quarter of the century, the family had relocated to the more agriculturally productive climes of southern Ontario. William married Mary Adams in 1893, the Ontario-born daughter of a Scottish immigrant who was also a William. Mary had more formal education than was the norm for a woman at that time and place, having attended a ladies college as the result of

an inheritance of cash and encouragement left to her by her father who died
while she was still in her teens. She was an independent spirit, not averse to
speaking her mind, and would play an instrumental role in encouraging young
Harold's educational pursuits.[1]

The family farm was one hundred acres in size and consisted of cultivated
land plus a woodlot. It was located in South Norwich Township, two miles
east of the small town of Otterville. Driving through the area today, we still
find farmland interspersed with old-growth forest. The primary difference
between then and now is the larger size of the farms currently operating.
Wheat and rye were the Innis family's initial cash crops, to be eventually superceded by livestock and dairy. Young Harold helped with the chores, of course,
but he was also an astute observer of the relationship between various levels of
agricultural production and the market constraints that affected them. Perhaps
it can be said that from the outset he had a systemic eye, one that would later
serve both his economic studies and his sense of the role of communications in
integrating social institutions and enabling empires. Not surprisingly he
excelled at school. The hodgepodge milieu of the one-room elementary
school he attended allowed him to learn with older children when the opportunity availed itself—and to earn the privilege of attending high school, especially when by 1905 there were three other siblings to help with the chores.

The high school was located in nearby Otterville, a hub for the immediate
region. The town was not unfamiliar to Innis. Regular Sunday visits to its
Spartan red-brick Baptist church (it has since been renovated and now bears a
United Church of Canada affiliation, which is an amalgam of the Congrega-
tionalist, Methodist, and Presbyterian churches) secured for a time Innis's faith
in the word of God, a faith that would be severely tested in the caldron of
World War I. Otterville has long since seceded its regional importance to centers better able to serve the interests of large agricultural operations. It remains
a sleepy burg, catering to retirees. A walk in the park overlooking the lake
yields one reminder of Innis's origins there: his name on a monument com-
memorating those residents of the township who had served in the Great War.

Otterville High School was the equivalent of what we would today call a
junior high school. Innis's success there eventually earned him an institutional
upgrade—to Woodstock Collegiate twenty miles to the north. Woodstock was
substantially larger than Otterville, but still a town whose primary raison d'être
was to center and serve an agricultural hinterland. The commute was daunting
but enlightening: walk to Otterville, catch the Grand Trunk Railway to
Woodstock, and then walk the remaining mile to school. Today, still located
where they were then, we find an expanded version of the old railway station
serving Woodstock, now a small city that bills itself as the "Dairy Capital of
Canada," and a rebuilt version of Woodstock Collegiate.

The railway journey to school cannot be taken for granted. What Innis learned from it might have been a catalyst inspiring his later doctoral dissertation and first book, *A History of the Canadian Pacific Railway*.[2] The workload he undertook in the distant school was rigorous and comprehensive. He graduated with aspirations of becoming a teacher. Unfortunately, the tuition cost plus the price of travel to and residence in a metropolis such as Toronto, where teacher certification could be attained, were at the time beyond his means. An alternative availed itself. He could field-test his pedagogical calling through an arrangement made by his father whereby Innis could teach in the old one-room Otterville schoolhouse, which was temporarily devoid of a certified instructor. Nervous at first, in time he deftly coped with a student body, diverse in age and ability, and with their parents.[3]

More worldly as a result of this experience, he decided to enter university—eventually to become a teacher, but for the moment to pursue a more general program of studies. Such an odyssey was now possible given the savings he had accrued from his uncertified teaching stint as well as from the hunting and trapping (mostly muskrats) he did during his downtime—still a child of the land, his second book would deal with the fur trade in Canada. He chose McMaster University, located then in Toronto, today in Hamilton, over the larger and more secular University of Toronto. It seemed, given its Baptist affiliation, an easier transition. Financial problems and self-doubt plagued his sojourn there, but the curriculum, especially history and political economy, along with the faculty, most notably James Ten Broeke and W. S. Wallace, inspired him.[4] Before his final year at McMaster, Innis taught summer school in rural Alberta, returning to Toronto with a newfound knowledge of the country and its railroad, which would provide groundwork for his future studies. He graduated in 1916 facing two prospects that would, in the best of all possible worlds, not be those he would want as options.

There was a war and many of his fellow students were enlisting. Innis put the possibility off until graduation. Familial pressure urged an alternative: the Baptist ministry, although he had yet to make the requisite declaration of faith necessary for the calling. He was, however, secure enough in his publicly undeclared religious beliefs to see it as a justification for the first option. He enlisted in the army as an infantryman and went to war. He saw the European conflict as a moral cause. "If I had no faith in Christianity, I don't think I would go," he told his sister.[5]

The war experience tested his fiber to the full. He also learned that the enemy across No Man's Land was not the only problem he and others like him had to face. According to Innis's son Donald, many Canadians who served became alienated in England as a result of the condescending and at times derisive attitude directed toward the "colonial" enlistees by British officers. In one incident that Innis observed involving Canadian soldiers unfamiliar with riding horseback, the officer in charge commented on their riding difficulties with reference to a Canadian national symbol by shouting repeatedly, "The maple leaves are falling."[6]

That he chose to serve in the signal corps may have significance in light of his later work in media history. World War I was a verifiable cross-section of the history of technology and communications, employing everything from pack animals to aircraft for transport, and carrier pigeons to the wireless for communication. After his arrival in France, he was sent to the front almost immediately and became a player in a major act: the battle of Vimy Ridge. While on a reconnaissance patrol, an artillery shell exploded close enough to seriously damage his leg. His war was over.

He convalesced in England before returning home. During that time, he read economics and, in response to the devastation the war was wreaking on a whole generation of young Canadians, worked on his master's thesis "The Returned Soldier," which was accepted by his alma mater, McMaster University. The next logical step, given the debating skills he honed while a university student, seemed to be a career in law, although he was still fascinated by economics. To satisfy this urge, he decided to spend the summer of 1918 at the University of Chicago studying the "dismal science." The subject, in the hands of one of his teachers, Frank Knight, was anything but. Innis was inspired, though far from satiated. The planned law career soon went on what would become a permanent hold and he enrolled full-time in the economics doctoral program.

There is something of a paradox surrounding his sojourn at the University of Chicago that continues to puzzle Innis commentators. The milieu was graced by two luminaries whose work helped inspire the nascent field of communication studies in the United States, George Herbert Mead and Robert Ezra Park. Marshall McLuhan has gone so far as to claim, in his foreword to the 1964 edition of Innis's *Bias of Communication,* that Innis was directly in their debt and "should be considered as the most eminent member of the Chicago school headed by Park."[7] James W. Carey has resisted rightly this attempted affiliation, pointing out that Innis did not study with Mead and Park while at Chicago, and that this tradition, or school, was on the wane when Innis turned his attention to communication-related research in the 1940s.[8] Nevertheless, Innis could not have been unaware of what was going on in such a heady milieu, especially since the work of Mead and Park was becoming known outside of their fields of social psychology and sociology, respectively. Some of Park's ideas regarding communication and community and his study of the press would later find their way into Innis's thinking on the relationship between media and social institutions.

During Innis's Windy City period, when his primary interest was in political economy and economic history, there was possibly another more immediate intellectual influence. America was discovering itself. Its history, geography, and literature were now deemed worthy of serious scholarly study. Canada had yet to make that leap. When it eventually did a decade later, Innis emerged as a key figure challenging the British-oriented European bias that had ruled the pedagogical roost since colonial times. Encouraging him in this direction was his doctoral supervisor at Chicago, the economic historian Chester W. Wright, who urged him to pursue a Canadian dissertation topic. "A History of the Canadian Pacific Railway" was the result. While at Chicago, Innis also got a chance to teach several introductory economics courses and saw in this experience the career that would later be his destiny. Part of that destiny included a fulfilling marriage to one of his former undergraduate students at Chicago, Mary Quayle. Mary's penchant for literature and the arts would help temper Innis's more hard-nosed social science inclinations. She also did significant research and publishing in a variety of areas. A much needed reappraisal of her contribution can be found in appendix B by J. David Black.

Just prior to graduating in 1920, Innis applied for teaching positions. He received offers from Beloit University in Illinois, Brandon College in Manitoba, and the University of Toronto. Toronto became his enthusiastic first choice—the second-most prestigious university (after McGill) in the country, in the second largest city (after Montreal). The faculty and facilities and the University of Toronto were not on a par with what he had encountered at Chicago, but he greatly appreciated being there. And, as is still the case with junior faculty in new academic postings, he labored assiduously to justify his worthiness to the faculty and to himself. He taught a range of courses, including one in an adult continuing education program in nearby Hamilton, did extensive committee work, and began to revise his doctorate for publication as a book. He revisited archives in Montreal and Ottawa, and no doubt reflected on his own past railway experiences. A welcome interlude to these endeavors occurred in 1921, following his first year of full-time teaching, when he married Mary that May in Chicago.

A History of the Canadian Pacific Railway was eventually published in 1923 by P. S. King and Son in London. What can we deduce from this work that might inform us where Innis was at, so to speak, intellectually in the early 1920s and what indications of his future thought are embedded in its turgid pages? The difficulty lies not in the text's conceptual intricacy—it is quite straightforward—nor does the book employ the bafflegab that is too often found in contemporary academic tomes. It is a challenging read primarily because of the exhaustive data mongering Innis felt was necessary to establish his argument.

Innis's *History of the Canadian Pacific Railway* deals with the development of

Canada's first transcontinental railway and the fortunes of the Canadian Pacific Railway (CPR) up to 1921. Details of the construction and operation of the line are presented using voluminous statistics and tables. High economic theory is eschewed in favor of a method that has been described as "descriptive and narrative."⁹ Innis himself referred to his approach as "evolutionary" and "scientific," no doubt as a way of legitimating the enormously empirical bent of his project. The book combines history and geography, and might be indebted to the tradition of American historical geography that was part of the milieu he had experienced at the University of Chicago.

The Canadian transcontinental railway has become part of the mythos of the nation, perhaps more so than the saga of the Union Pacific and Central Pacific Railroads in the United States, which bridged the nation in 1869. The Canadian project had to negotiate more formidable geographic barriers: muskeg in northern Ontario and treacherous mountain passes in the Rockies. It was not completed until 1886. In Canada, the story has been immortalized in the best-selling book *The National Dream: The Great Railway, 1871–1881* by Pierre Berton,¹⁰ which was eventually made into one of the most successful miniseries ever produced for Canadian television. It should be noted that at the time Innis wrote, in contrast to today, the general public in Canada knew very little about the CPR, and the situation was not much better in academe. Courses in Canadian history and geography were not *de rigueur*. This partly explains the comprehensiveness of Innis's study—the enormous detail we also find in the text is no doubt a legacy of the work having been a doctoral dissertation in its previous incarnation.

Innis begins by laying out the geographical infrastructure of the nation, which contained barriers the CPR had to overcome as well as the vectors through which the rail line would bridge east and west. Three formidable drainage basins had to be spanned: the Great Lakes and St. Lawrence River leading to the Atlantic Ocean in the east, the Arctic Ocean watershed through most of the prairies, and the Pacific Ocean drainage in the mountains of British Columbia. The difficulties of laying track in the west and frequent slowdowns were surmounted, he points out, by fears of American annexation of territory in that part of the country should Canada be perceived as a nation not unified by the strong transport and communication bond that a transcontinental rail line could provide.

The book also chronicles the government decisions involved in the CPR's history, the impact of the railway on outlying regions (especially with respect to wheat production and immigration on the prairies), and the profit and loss margin of the CPR over an extended period. The conclusion states what appears to be the obvious, that the railway had a profound impact on the "strength and character of the nation."¹¹ This seems patent today; it was not then. At the time, very little work was being done on Canadian history. When it was considered, mostly by European-trained commentators, the nation was deemed to have been formed through constitutional decisions and political leadership—Karl Marx used to refer to this kind of top-down historical approach as one in which royal decrees and statecraft were seen as prime movers. Innis probed deeper. He looked at land, commerce, labor, technology, transportation, and communication.

The CPR study also foreshadows concerns Innis would return to in his future work. He notes, for example, how monopolistic business interests in the east encouraged the far west to transport their goods by rail rather than by ship. And although rail was cheaper than a long ocean voyage, one consequence of that option was to diminish the west's independence, rendering it more vulnerable to decisions made in the urban centers of eastern Canada, "Western Canada has paid for the development of Canadian nationality, and it would appear that it must continue to pay. The acquisitiveness of eastern Canada shows little sign of abatement."[12]

Today, western Canada is known to be more resource rich than it was when Innis wrote—there is abundant oil and gas in Alberta and timber in British Columbia—but he was right when he intimated that resentment would persist regarding the power exerted by government and business interests in the east over the west. Every now and then, this resentment leads to talk of western separation (although the specter of a linguistically driven separation of Quebec, which is predominantly French speaking, is of greater concern to the Canadian government). Some in western Canada have even proposed joining with states in the Pacific Northwest to form a federation that would be called Cascadia. A diminution of the Canadian nation along such lines is one of the very things nineteenth-century politicians and business leaders believed construction of the CPR would help prevent. This theme, of the margins being dependent on, yet alienated from the center, recurs throughout Innis's studies in political economy. As we shall see, it resurfaces in his later work on the role of communications in establishing and maintaining empires. More immediately, the CPR study harbored the seeds of what would become Innis's next major project, and perhaps crowning achievement in political economy.

In assessing the importance of the railway, Innis concedes that prior to spikes and ties, paddles and portages made possible the fur trade, which helped open the land and encouraged immigration and agricultural development. Research for this project, which would culminate in 1930 with the publication of *The Fur Trade in Canada,* took him to archives, to be sure, but also beyond, to the land where the history he sought to study had been played out.[13] This was now possible given the permanent position he had secured in the Department of Political Economy at the University of Toronto, which offered him summer research opportunities. Hand in hand with the development of a Canadian-oriented pedagogical philosophy in economic history and theory came his acquaintance with a major aspect of his country's history. The fur trade project led him to do what might be called fieldwork, if such a term can be applied to economic history. In a deeper anthropological sense, the travels he undertook could also be construed as a vision quest, or the scholarly equivalent of a walkabout—a rite of passage that would lead him to the next level in his intellectual life's journey.

It began in earnest in 1924. Accompanied by longtime friend John Long, Innis began a backcountry journey that took them through the Northwest Territories and the Yukon, to the Mackenzie basin, and then down that river to the delta on the Beaufort Sea fringing the Arctic Ocean; this was two years before bush planes began serving the region. Some of the journey was done by

Innis on the Peace River (1924) during his voyage to research the history of the fur trade.

canoe—the leg from the Peace River to Lake Athabasca, and then down the Slave River to Great Slave Lake. A steam tug took them the remainder of the way, to Aklavik on the delta. His journal and correspondences describe the region, along with its inhabitants and their way of life. Minor annoyances, such as mosquitoes, foul weather, and relentless harassment by Indian dogs, are mentioned, yet archival photographs of him sitting in a canoe and on the deck of the tug suggest a relaxed persona in tune with his surroundings.

In 1926, he returned to the Yukon to look at mining and a year later he came back to study firsthand the mining, lumber, and pulp and paper industries of Nova Scotia, New Brunswick, Quebec, and northern Ontario. These research travels gave him a knowledge of the country few academics possessed and friends in many different walks of life. Traversing the fur trade routes also led him to alter notions that had underscored his CPR study. In that project, he saw the primary role of the railway as overcoming the limitations geography had imposed on the realization of Canadian nationhood. Although there was some hint in the book of what geographers sometimes call "possibilism," which might facilitate the transport link enabling Canadian unity—a mountain pass here or a river valley there—the land itself was seen largely as an obstacle to be overcome.

In reflecting earlier on the history of rail travel in Canada, he increasingly came to realize that some of the vectors assisting it were adjacent to waterways that had been used earlier by the fur trade. He also saw Confederation in 1867 (a date as revered by Canadians as 1776 is to Americans), which brought together the eastern provinces into the Dominion of Canada, as more than an act of political will. Nearly three centuries of exploration, commercial rivalries, and settlement linked to the fur trade had prefigured Confederation and the later incorporation of the western territories (now provinces). The waterways used for transport in extracting this staple resource and bringing supplies to those for whom it was directly or indirectly a source of livelihood were conduits through which had flowed the lifeblood of a gestating nation.

NOTES

1. Donald Grant Creighton, *Harold Adams Innis: Portrait of a Scholar* (1957; reprint, Toronto: University of Toronto Press, 1976), 6.

2. Harold A. Innis, *A History of the Canadian Pacific Railway* (1923; reprint, Toronto: University of Toronto Press, 1971).

3. Creighton, *Harold Adams Innis,* 18.

4. Ten Broeke's enigmatic query "Why do we attend to the things we attend?" would be cited at the outset of the preface of Innis's *The Bias of Communication* (1951; reprint, with an introduction by Paul Heyer and David Crowley, Toronto: University of Toronto Press,

1995). Wallace's constant reminder that even though the economic interpretation of history is not the only interpretation, it is the most profound, would remain an Innis maxim.

5. Quoted in Creighton, *Harold Adams Innis,* 31.

6. Interview in *Harold Innis: Patterns in Communication,* prod. and dir. Alison Beale, 52 min., 1990, videocassette.

7. Marshall McLuhan, foreword to *The Bias of Communication,* by Harold A. Innis (Toronto: University of Toronto Press, 1964), xvi.

8. James W. Carey, "Culture, Geography, and Communications: The Work of Harold Innis in an American Context," in *Culture Communication and Dependency: The Tradition of H. A. Innis,* ed. William Melody, Liora Salter, and Paul Heyer (Norwood, N.J.: Ablex, 1981). Carey explores Innis's relationship to the "Chicago School" in James W. Carey, "Innis 'in' Chicago: Hope As the Sire of Discovery," in *Harold Innis in the New Century: Reflections and Refractions,* ed. Charles R. Acland and William J. Buxton (Montreal: McGill-Queen's University Press, 1995).

9. Peter George, foreword to *A History of the Canadian Pacific Railway,* by Harold A. Innis (1923; reprint, Toronto: University of Toronto Press, 1971), v.

10. Pierre Berton, *The National Dream: The Great Railway, 1871–1881* (Toronto: McClelland and Stewart, 1970).

11. Innis, *History of the Canadian Pacific Railway,* 287.

12. Innis, *History of the Canadian Pacific Railway,* 294.

13. Harold A. Innis, *The Fur Trade in Canada* (1930; reprint, New Haven, Conn.: Yale University Press, 1962).

Chapter Two

From Fur to Fish

A violently fluctuating economy tends to produce inequalities and to create maladjustments which have serious consequences for the regions or classes most directly exposed to the effects of world competition.

—Harold A. Innis

Those who were aware of Innis's fur trade research sensed a great book was at hand. The first draft of *The Fur Trade in Canada* was completed in 1927. But completing it and getting it published were two separate things. He approached first his home institution, the University of Toronto, which balked at assisting in the publication of what in its first incarnation was most certainly a tome that in their estimation would be too costly to produce. Their fledgling press, however, did eventually consent to publish part of an anthology Innis had compiled in which some of his fur trade materials can be found, *Select Documents in Canadian Economic History*.[1] The fur trade manuscript itself he sent to P. S. King, who had published his CPR study. It agreed to publish this new manuscript, provided that a subsidy was available. It was not. Yale University Press said it would be interested in the project if several sections were deleted and the passages in French translated. He complied and the first edition was launched at the outset of the new decade.[2]

Innis's *The Fur Trade in Canada* is far more accessible in style than his first book. Facts, lists, and charts still abound, to be sure, but there is also more commentary to help readers make sense of these data. The work does have an intimidating comprehensiveness, which might lead contemporary readers accessing it for certain particulars to declare that Innis tells us more about the fur trade than we might want to know. But he also tells us many things about the industry and its history we should know. For example, that it is largely, though not wholly about the beaver. However, given *Castor canadensis*'s prominent role in birthing the industry, this is where he elects to begin. In chapter

1, therefore, the conceptual baseline is not the triad of classical political economy (land, labor, and capital), but organic nature. In succinct terms, he describes the beaver's physical features (especially its fur), preferred habitats, behavior, distribution, and engineering capabilities. This approach has overtones of the historiography of the eighteenth-century Enlightenment, which accommodated natural history into its purview.

The fur trade started, not with the intent of creating a major industry, but through incidental bartering with the Indians. One thing led to another. Demand for furs increased, requiring more formalized networks of acquisition. Although the fad for beaver hats eventually shifted the dominant market from Paris to London, it was still French traders who fueled it. These mobile entrepreneurs, known as *voyageurs,* pushed into the interior of the country in their birch-bark canoes. They discovered a plethora of aquatic highways that put them in contact with indigenous groups willing to trade. Since the beaver is not a prolific breeder, its destruction in one locality forced the economy and its effects deeper into the country. With the coming of winter, trade slowed but did not stop completely. As Innis points out, other forms of indigenous transportation appropriated by the Europeans came to the fore: the toboggan and snowshoes.

And what did the Indian peoples—who in Canada are now referred to as First Nations—get in return? A variety of European goods that included knives, axes, glass beads, combs, copper and iron kettles (which were highly prized), guns (which exacerbated intertribal warfare), and smallpox (which exacerbated genocide). Innis's dependency thesis—which in its classic formulation is used to assess the subservient position of the colonies with respect to wants emanating from the centers of European imperialist power—is used here to assess the crippling of indigenous cultures resulting from reliance on, perhaps addiction to is a more appropriate phrase, goods supplied to them by the colonists. The resulting intrusion disturbed the balance that had grown up prior to the coming of the Europeans. The new technology, with its radical innovations, brought about such a shift in the prevailing Indian culture that it led to the wholesale destruction of the peoples concerned by warfare and disease.[3]

Unfortunately, Innis did not give this line of inquiry the further attention he seems to imply it deserves. Later writers would delve more deeply into the plight of the First Nations under contact. Of note is the work of another Canadian, Ronald Wright, who speaks eloquently to the topic.[4]

The story of the fur trade in Canada as chronicled by Innis is also the story of corporate rivalries and what we might call a hostile takeover. The Northwest Company pushed westward into the far reaches of the country and depended heavily on First Nations middlemen to broker trade. The Hudson's Bay Company set up large trading posts on the shores of and rivers draining into the

Hudson and James Bays. This fostered direct barter with the various tribes that could bring their goods to the trading posts. It also facilitated shipping the goods directly to Europe during the ice-free months, thereby bypassing reliance on eastern ports (mainly Montreal) located along the St. Lawrence River. Rivalry between the two companies, which occasionally prompted physical attacks, led to an amalgamation on March 26, 1821, "The geographic advantages of the Hudson's Bay Company were merged with the type of organization which had developed in the French *régime* and which had been elaborated with such effectiveness in the Northwest Company."[5]

The name Hudson's Bay Company was retained during the merger and is now the one most Canadians recall when they reflect on the history of the country. Yet, according to Innis, it was the Northwest Company that built up an organization from the Atlantic to the Pacific that "provided the foundations for the present Dominion of Canada. . . . It was the forerunner of Confederation . . . and built on the work of the French *voyageurs,* the contributions of the Indian, especially the canoe and pemmican [dried lean meat, usually buffalo, ground and mixed with fat, which preserves without refrigeration, and berries], and the organizing ability of the Anglo-American merchants."[6]

In studying the fur trade, Innis notes how it was both preceded and followed by the exploitation of two other staple resources that shaped the country: fish and lumber. Before the fur trade began, he notes, the "abundance of cod to be caught off the Grand Banks of Newfoundland and in the territory adjacent to the Gulf of St. Lawrence led the peoples concerned to direct their energy to a pursuit of the fishing industry."[7] In *The Cod Fisheries: The History of an International Economy,* he further explores this industry.[8] During the 1930s, he wrote several essays that built on the geography of transport he had studied with respect to the fur trade. They deal with how major waterways used in that industry were later adapted to the exploitation of a staple resource, lumber, that remains integral to the Canadian economy. In the conclusion to *The Fur Trade in Canada,* he had already begun looking in this direction: "The lumber industry was largely responsible, directly and indirectly, for the improvement of waterways and for the construction of railways prior to Confederation."[9]

The historical approach Innis employed, both in his economic and in his later communication studies, is one in which individuals, almost in a Marxian sense, are the agents of broader institutional patterns and processes, but not completely. One outgrowth of the fur trade research that is almost never mentioned in commentaries is his *Peter Pond: Fur Trader and Adventurer.*[10] It is an elegantly produced little book—153 fully cut pages with two-inch margins framing the text and a period map. It is engaging and accessible to a general readership and redeems the legacy of a major player in the fur trade whom history has overlooked.

Peter Pond (1740–1807), who hailed from and eventually died in Milford, Connecticut, worked for the Northwest Company and was the first white man to reach the Mackenzie basin. His contributions, however, have been downplayed by none other than Sir Alexander Mackenzie himself, a major figure in Canadian history—most Canadian school children are aware of Mackenzie, while few Canadian academics have even heard of Pond. Innis argues that this should not be the case. He quotes extensively and comments from the journals of Pond, parts of which were destroyed and the rest disregarded because of perceived deficiencies in Pond's writing ability. To the contemporary eye and ear, Pond's prose seems that of a person who is literate but not well read. It retains, both in terms of grammar and spelling, an oral and phonetic quality. One can almost hear Pond's voice when reading "lake Mishegan . . . We sun imbarkt . . . beaing destatute myself . . . convars with the other tribes nor intermarey" and so on.

For Innis, Pond is as reputable a chronicler as those among his peers who have been more privileged by subsequent historical acceptance. The last phrase in the previous quotes also reveals, as Innis notes, "that the fur trader was also an anthropologist."[11] No doubt during his research journeys he occasionally saw himself in a similar light.

As Innis researched and published, he rose through the ranks of academe, but not without a struggle. Although promotion to assistant professor in 1925 was a virtual formality, achieving the rank of associate that he applied for four years later was not. An account of what transpired reveals his character and his self-confidence.[12] The head of the department of political economy, an Oxford-trained classicist and philosopher, who probably saw the American-trained Innis as nothing more than a workmanlike empirical researcher, did not promote him. Insult followed injustice when a junior colleague with a far less distinguished record received the promotion he sought. Innis did not complain or appeal, he simply resigned.

At this point in his career, a position at an American university would almost certainly have been an option. Fortunately, university officials soon saw the error of their ways and offered him the promotion. He accepted, but not without a degree of bitterness, "The row is over temporarily and I get my promotion to Associate Professor. I am not particularly pleased with it since it was got by sheer brute strength and I don't think a university should be conducted on that basis."[13] Can we not possibly surmise that the disrespect showed toward him prompted a déjà vu recalling the attitudes he and other Canadian soldiers had faced during the war at the hands of British officers?

Later promotions went more smoothly, to full professor in 1936, head of the department in 1937, and dean of the graduate school in 1947. Apart from the painful blip in his academic trajectory that occurred in 1929, he published two important essays that year. The first, "The Teaching of Economic History in Canada,"[14] is an outgrowth of the way his research and course development had unfolded since the start of his appointment at the University of Toronto. He argues that economic history should be the core of Canadian economics. Models that have been applied to other industrialized countries, such as the United States and Great Britain, the sources for most textbooks then in use in Canada, have a very limited utility. His plea for a distinctively Canadian textbook addressing his concerns that could be used in secondary schools and universities would be answered by none other than his wife, Mary (see appendix B). This is not to say that Canadian economics texts were unavailable when he was developing his courses in the 1920s. Several were, but their orientation was practical rather than theoretical. American sources, although not without some applicability, tended to lean too heavily on the frontier thesis espoused by Frederick Jackson Turner. Innis believed this thesis, which saw the gradual settlement of a semiautonomous frontier as a key to nation building, did not apply to Canada where the frontier was controlled by the dictates of an imperial metropole hungry for staple resources.

The essay also makes a plea for an association and journal of economic history. And that, too, like Mary's textbook, would come to pass—he would be instrumental in establishing both. As for a general economics curriculum for Canadian universities, he was far from being a chauvinist. Courses included a general introduction to economic history, French economic history in the seventeenth and eighteenth centuries, the British Empire after 1763, the industrial revolution in other countries, including the United States, and Canadian economic history. In addition, students were expected to have a basic grasp of French, German, Latin, biology, geology, electricity, metallurgy, and mechanics. Today, few economics programs anywhere are so comprehensive. Perhaps more should be.

Finally, he insists that we "cannot pretend to an understanding of Canadian economic history without an adequate history of transportation," which must include studying the crucial role of water transport with respect to fish and fur, and the importance of the railway in terms of staples, such as wheat, minerals, lumber, and pulp and paper.[15] Given that in a large segment of the history he studied transportation was also the main means of communication, can we not see this as an anticipation of his later work in that field? More evidence is forthcoming when he notes how inland waterways favored movement of a light valuable commodity such as fur, where primary waterways were effective carriers of bulk commodities such as lumber and minerals. He would, over a decade later, think of media in similar if not identical terms: those that are light and portable (e.g., papyrus and paper) favoring an emphasis on space, and more durable or expensive media (e.g., stone or parchment) imparting a time-bias to the societies that employed them. Another bridge in this 1929 essay to his future work is even more direct, "The rapid rise of advertising has been largely responsible for the development of the pulp and paper industry."[16]

As Innis developed his pedagogical mandate for political economy based on a thorough integration of economic history, he also sought theoretical sources whose explanatory power might enhance the discipline as he conceived it. No theorist became more influential to him during this segment of his career, as well as to his later communications work, than the American Thorstein Veblen (1857–1929). Veblen is the clown prince in the pantheon of great economic thinkers, a maverick and an iconoclast. His *Theory of the Leisure Class: An Economic Study in the Evolution of Institutions* took no prisoners and rocketed him to both fame and infamy. The *Theory of Business Enterprise* and later publications added inertia to his reputation.[17]

Veblen was like Innis in that he came from a farm background (in Minnesota) and attained an academic career. He was completely unlike Innis in terms of personality. A notorious womanizer and bane of administrators, Veblen cut a swath through several universities—one of them being Chicago two decades before Innis arrived there. His work spawned cult followers who saw him as a seer, critics who dismissed him as a buffoon, and a general readership who regarded him as an astute satirist—he coined the term "conspicuous consumption"—rather than as a major economic thinker.

Knowing, in 1929, that Veblen's scholarly career was over—Veblen himself had declared this to be so—Innis undertook a thoughtful and balanced appraisal of the legacy. It was published in the *Southwestern Political and Social Science Quarterly* only months before Veblen died. What others saw as satire in Veblen, Innis deemed to be a fearlessness coupled with the use of irony on the part of an economist who was the first to "attempt a general stock-taking of general tendencies in a dynamic society saddled with machine industry, just as Adam Smith was the first to present a general stock-taking before machine industry came in."[18] No small praise from someone who was familiar with all of Veblen's work and well aware of its various shortcomings. The aspects of Veblen that most profoundly influenced Innis included the integration of economic history and theory, with the former a necessary precondition for the latter; also the way Veblen studied processes of growth and decay in society, which Innis applied to his study of staples and incorporated into his later examination of the role of communications in the rise and fall of civilizations; and finally Veblen's study of the effects of machine industry, which informed Innis's later critical work dealing with mechanization and mass culture.

The decade that culminated in *Fur Trade* would be followed by one whose capstone became *Cod Fisheries*. Each of these major research projects had to compete, to the degree that time would allow, with a variety of other activities

Innis was pursuing. In the 1920s, he had sought to develop a curriculum appropriate to the way he conceived political economy. In the 1930s, with that largely accomplished, he explored various branch lines of his staples research—mining, lumber, and pulp and paper. He regularly lent his expertise to various government committees and began to assume the role of a public intellectual. Travel was also on the agenda. As was the case with the fur trade research, the cod project inspired him to visit some of the places of which he wrote. In the late spring of 1930, he therefore journeyed to Newfoundland and Labrador.

Several research papers soon followed. In a 1931 paper, "The Rise and Fall of the Spanish Fishing Industry in Newfoundland," he looks at early European attempts to establish a fishing industry in an area teeming with cod.[19] Despite the abundance of the resource, international rivalries resulted. Spain became for a time the major player, outperforming and outmaneuvering the Portuguese, French, and Irish, who had made earlier inroads. By the sixteenth century, open conflict was not unusual. Innis notes that following the defeat of the Spanish Armada in 1597 and the Peace of 1604, Spain's supremacy in the industry was eclipsed by Britain, which in turn was able to export cod to Spain, further internationalizing the economy. In recent years, conflict has arisen once again. A moratorium on cod to revive dwindling stocks has been violated by several nations. Ships have been seized in both international and Canadian territorial waters leading to strained relations between Canada and Spain.

Ultimately, France supplanted Spain as Britain's chief rival, but its approach to the industry was different. In the 1931 paper "An Introduction to the Economic History of the Maritimes, Including Newfoundland and New England,"[20] Innis points out that the French fished over a wide area from ports scattered along its coast, with the catch intended for domestic consumption. In contrast, Protestant England's declining domestic market for fish led to a trade-oriented approach that was more circumscribed: from the West Country emerged fleets that established their base of operations on a small part of Newfoundland known as the Avalon Peninsula, which "became in some sense the cornerstone of the British Empire from the point of territory, trade, shipping, seamen, industry, agriculture and finances."[21] The degree to which Newfoundland could develop, however, was limited by a short season, compounded by poor agriculture and lumber. The situation was much better in New England and by the nineteenth century the United States established a strong foothold in the industry, which it now extended southward. Interestingly, Innis uses this example to challenge Turner's frontier thesis. He argues against the view that the Appalachians were a formidable barrier to be overcome by claiming that the real pull on New England was not toward the land but out to the sea, thereby applying his staples thesis to part of American history.

Research papers such as these, which were usually presented first at conferences and then published soon after, made Innis a facilitator and focal point for
scholars in Canada as well as in the United States. Wherever he traveled, be it
for purposes of research or to present a paper, he always made it a point to visit
the local campuses to find out who was doing what. Although he was trained
as an economist, his interests prompted him to see no firm boundaries between
disciplines. He presented his papers in whatever disciplinary conference he
thought might benefit from his work, thereby becoming an early proponent
of interdisciplinarity. He did not, as some later devotees suggested, advocate
the abolishment of conventional disciplinary parameters, but he did insist that
there are occasionally points of focal overlap, or common ground, between
disciplines that can provide a basis for intellectual cross-fertilization.

An early example of his interdisciplinarity can be found in the paper "Transportation As a Factor in Canadian Economic History," which was presented
to the Canadian Political Science Association in 1931.[22] It is, of course, as the
title suggests, economic history, but is presented in such a way as to be of interest to the audience of political scientists he was addressing at the time. The
perspective also invites interest from geographers and sociologists; today, media
historians might find parts of the essay relevant. The paper distills a major
theme that recurs throughout his early work: the importance of transportation.
He begins by talking about the sea routes used in fishing and the geology of
the country as it relates to the formation of the lakes, rivers, and bays used in
the fur trade, lumber industry, and general intracontinental transport. The Erie
Canal in New York State is seen as prompting Canadian development of the
Welland Canal connecting Lakes Erie and Ontario to facilitate access from the
upper lakes to major ports along the St. Lawrence River. With the coming of
rail travel, it initially worked in tandem with the waterways. This created what
he calls "the beginning of the amphibious stage in the history of transport."[23]
Eventually, as rail travel expanded, and with inland travel by waterways impossible in winter, this amphibious stage was supplanted by a "land stage" dominated by the railway.

Other papers at other conferences followed throughout the decade, as did
various editorial projects. Notable among them was a series of conferences and
publications sponsored by the Carnegie Endowment for International Peace,
titled The Relations of Canada and the United States, under the general editor-
ship of James T. Shotwell. Innis attended the first conference, which was held
in New York City in the summer of 1932, and later edited and wrote prefaces
for the four-volume series, which had been authored by Canadians, and contributed his own volume with the publication of Cod Fisheries in 1940. He
insisted and received freedom to be an editor in his own way, taking advice,
but not explicit directions from Shotwell. An inkling of what he gleaned from

working on the project can be seen in the 1938 paper "Economic Trends in Canadian-American Relations."[24]

Speaking to a largely American audience, he urges that U.S. economic policies take Canada into account before being implemented, since to do so could provide long-term benefits to both countries. He discusses Canada's dependency relationship to the United States, whereby it exports staples, such as pulp and paper and minerals, and imports manufactured goods, especially machines of various kinds. Another import Innis notes, which took on greater importance when media studies preoccupied him, was radio, a medium that "crosses boundaries which stopped the press."[25] Overly close economic ties of the dependent kind with the United States, he argues, had the effect of weakening Canada politically in relation to Europe, which was not to the benefit of North America as a whole. The paper ends with a plea for closer cooperation between the two countries by citing a passage from Winnie the Pooh that deals with the value of shared decision making in the economics of food consumption. This is an early example of Innis the humorist, a trait that would be increasingly evident in subsequent writings.

The Canadian-American project was the first of several that raised the prominence of Innis and other social scientists in the eyes of the Canadian government. The result was service in an advisory capacity as a member of various royal commissions. The Great Depression had seized hold of the country and policies needed to be implemented that would lessen its stranglehold. Innis took the position of a cautious reformer, always leery of the motives of government. He was equally leery of those, including some of his colleagues whom he called "hot gospellers," who advocated the implementation of more drastic nationalist and socialist measures. One of those hot gospellers was a colleague of Innis's in the history department, Frank Underhill, who argued that class conflict and a crisis in capitalism underscored the malaise of the times. He advocated an immediate social restructuring. Innis may have been sympathetic with Underhill's diagnosis, but not with the proposed cure. Needless to say, Underhill's views made administrators uncomfortable, and some were outraged when on the eve of World War II he questioned a reflexive loyalty to the British Empire, arguing that the Canadian national interest had priority. A minor media event resulted and the university was pressured to seek Underhill's dismissal. Innis came to his defense with a carefully worded letter that highlighted Underhill's service to his country in World War I and implied that if academic freedom were breached and Underhill fired, the university might be facing Innis's resignation as well.[26]

In 1932 and 1933, Innis visited western Canada to see what impact the Depression had on the prairies, which shared the dust bowl conditions plaguing several U.S. Midwestern states. In 1933, he also went to England to participate in a conference on international relations and to further pursue his fish research. In 1934, he was appointed to a royal commission to study the economy of Nova Scotia and authored a telling report. The next year, he traveled to the other end of the country to teach a summer course at the University of British Columbia in Vancouver. In 1936, he received his full professorship. Three notable events followed in 1937. First, he edited *The Dairy Industry in Canada*,[27] for which he provided the lead essay "An Introduction to Canadian Economic Studies."[28] This only served to compound the stress he was experiencing from so many diverse commitments. Before the term "workaholic" had been coined, Innis became one of its victims. That March he became bedridden with what was diagnosed as "nervous exhaustion."[29] The summer following his recovery, he was appointed head of the Department of Political Economy, and he resumed his full workload along with a new set of responsibilities.

Shortly after donning his new mantle of formal academic leadership, Innis honored two retiring colleagues with Festschrifts, editing both volumes; contributed several essays to anthologies compiled by others; and perhaps most importantly, managed to complete, in typically Innisian fashion, a sprawling and overly detailed first draft of the codfish study. Substantial revision was necessary, and after securing the editorial assistance of Arthur E. McFarlane, he plunged ahead. Honorific interruptions, however, were still a regular occurrence. In 1938, he was appointed president of the Canadian Political Science Association. His inaugural address, "The Penetrative Powers of the Price System," was given that May. Political scientists were given a lesson in the monetary aspects of economic history since the sixteenth century and its effect on trade and settlement. The argument is dense and covers a vast terrain. It also jumps from one topic to the next and is laced with aphorisms, thereby anticipating the format his later communications writings would employ. Another glimpse of an aspect of the later work can be seen in a lengthy paragraph on radio, part of which is worth citing:

> Competition between newspapers and the radio for advertising, as well as in the handling of news, has been evident in the concerted attack by the press on the Canadian Broadcasting Corporation following contracts with American firms. From the standpoint of the public it is a choice between Moon Mullins and Charlie McCarthy. The radio capitalizes the disadvantage of the large newspaper in appealing to stereotypes which refuse to be blurred, as is evident in the strength of religion in the rural areas. While it has served the dictatorship of Russia, Italy, Germany and Japan, it has assisted the provincialism of Mr. Aberhardt and the federalism of Mr. Roosevelt. As a new invention the radio threatens to circumvent the walls imposed by tariffs and to reach across boundaries frequently denied to other media of communication.[30]

Some of the essays Innis contributed at this time to anthologies he did not edit himself dealt with staples other than fur and fish. The importance of lumber, wheat, and mining merited, if not book-length studies, certainly condensed overviews. In "The Lumber Trade in Canada,"[31] he notes how major rivers that had been used in the fur trade were adapted to transport lumber (raw logs). Industrialism and urban growth escalated the demand for wood. In the United States, the rapidly expanding network of canals and railways facilitated transport to major markets. Timber (logs cut and squared in Canadian mills) went to Great Britain. Something Innis stresses here and elsewhere is that these ships did not return empty. They were instrumental in bringing immigrants to the country.

Eventually, the industry moved west, to the rich forest regions of British Columbia. Innis describes how this happened using an almost aphoristic turn of phrase, "On the St. Lawrence the timber trade brought immigration and in British Columbia immigration brought the timber trade."[32] In the west, this resource was exploited using more expansive technology and larger sawmills. By the turn of the century, Pacific rim countries became trading partners and with the opening of the Panama Canal in 1914, British Columbia timber was shipped globally. Lumber is seen today as a renewable resource—although old growth forest cannot be fully replaced after it is cut—a concept that did not exist at the time Innis wrote. He notes that after a region is exhausted, mills are abandoned and ghost towns often result. Logging is also an industry that he points out has been subject to strong provincial control, just the opposite of the more federally overseen staple that became an economic mainstay of central Canada: wheat.

In "The Wheat Economy,"[33] he traces the history of this staple. The saga is a complex one. Industrialization increased the population of metropolitan areas, thereby creating a demand for wheat, which in turn prompted migration to the prairies to exploit the abundant land and rich soil favorable to extensive wheat farming. However, then as now, many variables were at play and the price of wheat fluctuated, often dramatically. Factors such as alternative food preferences, other market sources for wheat, along with yields that varied from year to year (especially during the Depression), all contributed. One consequence of this instability was migration from the prairies to eastern Canada and the United States (made more difficult after 1930) and the shift to relatively more predictable livestock and dairy farming.

One outgrowth of Innis's involvement in researching the history of wheat production on the prairies was another project, such as the *Peter Pond* study, that demonstrated his interest in the role of the individual in history. In 1940, he published *The Diary of Alexander James McPhail*.[34] Alexander James McPhail (1885–1937) became a key figure in one of the most significant organizations

to emerge from the cooperative movement on the Canadian prairies, the Sas-
katchewan Wheat Pool. The diary chronicles McPhail's attempts to unify
farmers in the face of numerous political and commercial obstacles. Innis does
far more here than merely present McPhail's diary. He functions as a selective
biographer, providing a general introduction, introductions to each chapter,
intertextual commentaries within the chapters, and a conclusion (which he sees
as provisional) that assesses McPhail's place in the agricultural history of the
prairies. One sees in McPhail's background certain elements—family farm
upbringing, interest in education, and qualities of leadership—that Innis must
have identified with and drawn him toward his subject.

Nonorganic staples were also of interest to Innis at this time. In his essay
"The Canadian Mining Industry,"[35] he assesses how precious metals, such as
gold, which had once lured Spain to the New World, became important to the
North American economy. Initially, this occurred with its discovery in California in 1849, but shortly thereafter, British Columbia yielded goldfields, and by
the turn of the century the Klondike became a major producing (perhaps
promising more than actually producing) region.

At the opposite end of the mineral spectrum from gold was coal. Canada
had substantial deposits in Nova Scotia and British Columbia, but they paled
in significance to the massive reserves in Pennsylvania. Unfortunately for Canada, the places where coal was found did not have the capacity to industrialize,
as was the case in the United States. Innis describes succinctly the factors at
play, "The heavy, bulky, and cheap character of coal gave it a dominant place
in the location of industrial growth. . . . Metallic ores move more cheaply to
coal than coal to ore."[36] Canada, of course, possesses its share of metallic
resources, such as iron, nickel, lead, zinc, and copper, which could be "moved
to coal." Nevertheless, the mining operations necessary for their extraction, as
Innis observes, have depended heavily on American capital. The importance
of coal was eventually superceded by oil, to which Innis only gives passing
mention. However, researchers building on his legacy have since turned their
attention to that staple as well.[37]

In September 1939, Innis was putting the finishing touches on the codfish
manuscript when Germany invaded Poland, which precipitated World War II.
The book appeared a year later and provides a finale to a decade of research in
a way analogous to how *Fur Trade* brought home his 1920s' research odyssey.
His *Cod Fisheries* is a multinational study. Note that he subtitles the book "*The
History*," whereas his CPR study was deemed to be "*A History*." Perusal of
Cod Fisheries, however, shows that intellectual modesty regarding the title
would have been inappropriate. The scope and detail are overwhelming. One
senses, as Innis must have sensed in writing it, that this would be the last word
on the subject. In a foreword to the volume, Shotwell describes the book as "a

challenge to the imagination and insight of the reader." He might have added "patience," given the enormous mass of data and multinational histories contained in the work's five-hundred-plus pages. The fact of Shotwell's foreword, and Innis's grateful acknowledgment of his support in the preface, derives from the book being part of the "Canada and the United States" series they had been working on since 1932.

Chapter 1 immediately draws our attention to the importance of the book's subject matter, "No other industry has engaged the activities of any people in North America over such a long period of time and in such restricted areas."[38] Innis then begins his assessment of it the same way he commenced his study of the fur trade: with nature itself. To know the industry we must know the object it seeks. We therefore learn of the cod, a rich, fleshy but not fatty repository of protein that teemed in great numbers on the continental shelf of northeast North America, especially in the area east of Newfoundland known as the Grand Banks. The banks, located between the warm Gulf Stream and the cold Labrador Current, were a piscatorial Valhalla. We learn about the habits, diet, and preferred locations for *Gadus morhua,* a food staple that could, before the days of canning and refrigeration, be transported great distances when salted or dried.

It all started with John Cabot in 1497. A Venetian in the service of England's Henry VII, Cabot was commissioned to find what had eluded Christopher Columbus: a sea route to Asia. Instead, he "discovered" North America, at least the northern part of it. The coastal regions he surveyed were sparse and uninviting. But offshore, as indicated in a report of the expedition that Innis cites, "the sea there is swarming with fish, which can be taken not only with the net but in baskets let down with a stone, so that it sinks in the water."[39] This discovery has since been vividly dramatized on Canadian television in a "Heritage Minute," a sad reminder of a time, five centuries before the current moratorium, when cod seemed to be an inexhaustible resource.

Despite this discovery of the Grand Banks, the English were still content to use Iceland as a fish provider. The French and Portuguese were not so slow in casting their nets. They made significant inroads in exploiting the new fishing grounds. That it could yield a rich harvest was clear to the English as a result of catches they had plundered from French ships. Enter Spain, and here Innis goes over and amplifies material that he covered in the 1931 paper already cited. With the decline of the Spanish fishing industry in the early seventeenth century, France and England became the major players. Because the English had little salt and a more limited home market for fish than the French, their industry was a "dry fishery," which necessitated that land adjacent to the fishing grounds be used to dry the catch. This resulted in the settlement of Newfoundland, which in turn became a jumping-off point for the establishment of a New England fishery. This second fishery eventually expanded south, to the West Indies and the coast of South America.

During much of the eighteenth century, the New England fishery competed with the Newfoundland operation for skilled labor and access to markets. The French were still a factor, and although their rights to fish the Grand Banks were curtailed by the Treaty of Utrecht in 1713, concessions were made in 1763 whereby they were ceded St. Pierre and Miquelon and were permitted to establish a strong presence in the Gaspé (in eastern Quebec). Following the American Revolution—Innis sees commercial rivalry between Britain and New England as a major catalyst in the American desire for independence—the Peace of Versailles in 1783 granted New England access to the Grand Banks. The nineteenth century saw the emergence of Nova Scotia as a major base for an industry that now saw mackerel and herring challenge, but not usurp, the supremacy of cod. Eventually, with the development of industrial capitalism and an economy that looked to the land rather than the sea, the overall importance of fishing waned and the regions in Canada where it once thrived became economically disadvantaged, a situation that continues to the present day.

This sketch fails to do justice to the complexity of Innis's analysis. His arguments are not always, in fact are rarely easy to follow, largely because of the diversity of the connections he makes. The codfish industry, as he argues, was about more than fish. It led to international rivalries as well as commercial rivalries within nations. This led to the opening of trade routes (that served as lines of transportation and communication), settlements, monopolies, wars, treaties, and economic policies among a diversity of nations. And once again, as he did with Pond and the fur trade and McPhail's role in the history of prairie wheat pools, Innis shows an acute sense of the role of the individual in history. Eight years after the publication of *Cod Fisheries,* Innis edited the multivolume *The Diary of Simeon Perkins.*[40] Simeon Perkins (1735–1812), who hailed from Norwich, Connecticut, became a major figure in the Nova Scotia fishing business in the late eighteenth and early nineteenth centuries. His diary evidences everything from the nitty-gritty of production, markets, and prices, to political commentary. It was so useful to Innis during his cod research that he eventually deemed it merited publication.

During the 1920s and 1930s, Innis gave fur and fish most of his scholarly attention. However, his work in political economy and staples research did not end in 1940 with the publication of *Cod Fisheries,* despite the diversity of interests that characterized the years to follow. That he influenced the students he taught during his first two decades in academe is without question, but we must remember that he was teaching economic history to students who were preparing for careers in commerce and finance. It was only after this period that he became an icon and attracted a coterie of graduate students.[41]

During the 1930s, he was also instrumental, although certainly not the only one, to further the cause of what is now referred to as Canadian studies. Within Canada, the staples thesis, connecting as it does many strands in the development of the country, functions in ways that are similar to how Innis would see communication media in his later work. In both projects, we have a concern for the nature and characteristics of the medium in question, be it fur or fish, clay or papyrus, along with an analysis of the networks that exploit it in the service of a center, or metropole, to whose interests the producing regions must serve by remaining marginal and dependent.

Innis did not discover this process in Canadian history. But he did show how it underscored the political and constitutional edifice that many had seen as that country's prime mover. Although his later work is characterized as both materialist and idealist, the staples research is clearly the former. As William Westfall notes, "Instead of recounting the gradual unfolding of an idea or series of ideas (such as political liberty, responsible government, or autonomy) . . . it turned history toward the study of the ongoing ramifications of a body of material factors in a geopolitical and economic setting."[42]

This brings to mind and suggests parallels with Karl Marx's notion of an economic base, or infrastructure, supporting a historically derived superstructure. Innis, however, seems to have avoided Marxian theory. Certainly he did not truck with socialism. In a 1948 essay, he makes reference to the limits of a Marxian approach and claims to be using "the Marxian interpretation to interpret Marx."[43] A worthy undertaking to be sure, but he never fulfills the promise of such an analysis anywhere in his published writings. It is also worth noting that he uses the term "Marxian" rather than "Marxist," which implies the source rather than the tradition that sprang from it. Although class conflict and a concept of ideology, both mainstays of Marxian analysis, are absent from Innis's staples research, material conditions of production and a sense of the cyclical nature of history (which Marx inherited from Georg Hegel) are clearly present—interestingly, Innis's later work valorizing the oral tradition (see chapter 5) reads like a cultural addendum to Marx's notion of primitive communism.

More detailed, if unintentional parallels between Marx and Innis have been argued by economic theorists.[44] Nevertheless, it seems likely that the source for whatever Marxian ideas seeped into Innis's staples research derives from the economist he most revered: Thorstein Veblen. Veblen, unlike Innis, confronted Marx directly, taking what he needed while jettisoning the rest.

To explore the influence of the staples theory on contemporary political economy is beyond the scope or mandate of this book. Following Innis's death, Canadian history, although revering his legacy, moved more toward biographical and social approaches, while political economy has continued for the most part to champion neoclassical research strategies augmented by econometrics. There are, however, growing signs of a revival of interest in his earlier staples research among a current generation of Canadian scholars.[45] In the United States, Innis's economic work has attracted a small following among historians of New England who find resonance in his history of the fishing industry. Most recently, those who study both the plight of underdeveloped nations in the postcolonial Third World and globalization are recognizing that Innis's approach to political economy has much to offer.

NOTES

1. Harold A. Innis, ed., *Select Documents in Canadian Economic History* (Toronto: University of Toronto Press, 1929).

2. Harold A. Innis, *The Fur Trade in Canada* (1930; reprint, New Haven, Conn.: Yale University Press, 1962).

3. Innis, *Fur Trade in Canada,* 389.

4. Ronald Wright, *Stolen Continents: The Americas through Indian Eyes since 1492* (Boston: Houghton Mifflin, 1992).

5. Innis, *Fur Trade in Canada,* 280.

6. Innis, *Fur Trade in Canada,* 262.

7. Innis, *Fur Trade in Canada,* 384.

8. Harold A. Innis, *The Cod Fisheries: The History of an International Economy* (1940; reprint, Toronto: University of Toronto Press, 1954).

9. Innis, *Fur Trade in Canada,* 396.

10. Harold A. Innis, ed., *Peter Pond: Fur Trader and Adventurer* (Toronto: Irwin and Gordon, 1930).

11. Innis, *Peter Pond,* 36.

12. Donald Grant Creighton, *Harold Adams Innis: Portrait of a Scholar* (1957; reprint, Toronto: University of Toronto Press, 1978).

13. Quoted in Creighton, *Harold Adams Innis,* 71.

14. In Harold A. Innis, *Essays in Canadian Economic History,* ed. Mary Q. Innis (Toronto: University of Toronto Press, 1962).

15. Innis, *Essays in Canadian Economic History,* 12.

16. Innis, *Essays in Canadian Economic History,* 15.

17. Thorstein Veblen, *Theory of the Leisure Class: An Economic Study in the Evolution of Institutions* (New York: Macmillan, 1899); Thorstein Veblen, *Theory of Business Enterprise* (New York: Scribner's, 1904).

18. Harold A. Innis, "The Work of Thorstein Veblen," reprinted in Innis, *Essays in Canadian Economic History,* 25.

19. Reprinted in Innis, *Essays in Canadian Economic History.*

20. Reprinted in Innis, *Essays in Canadian Economic History.* Canada's Maritime provinces

are New Brunswick, Nova Scotia, Prince Edward Island, and Newfoundland. The latter attained provincial status only in 1949, or eighteen years after Innis wrote the essay.

21. Innis, *Essays in Canadian Economic History*, 31.

22. Reprinted in Innis, *Essays in Canadian Economic History*.

23. Innis, *Essays in Canadian Economic History*, 69.

24. Reprinted in Innis, *Essays in Canadian Economic History*.

25. Innis, *Essays in Canadian Economic History*, 236.

26. Eric Havelock, *Harold A. Innis: A Memoir* (Toronto: The Harold Innis Foundation, 1982), 21.

27. Harold A. Innis, ed., *The Dairy Industry in Canada* (Toronto: Ryerson, 1937).

28. Reprinted in Innis, *Essays in Canadian Economic History*.

29. Creighton, *Harold Adams Innis*, 95.

30. Innis, *Essays in Canadian Economic History*, 268.

31. Reprinted in Innis, *Essays in Canadian Economic History*.

32. Innis, *Essays in Canadian Economic History*, 245.

33. Reprinted in Innis, *Essays in Canadian Economic History*.

34. Harold A. Innis, ed., *The Diary of Alexander James McPhail* (Toronto: University of Toronto Press, 1940).

35. Reprinted in Innis, *Essays in Canadian Economic History*.

36. Innis, *Essays in Canadian Economic History*, 315.

37. For example, see Arlon R. Tussing, "Implications of Oil and Gas Development for Alaska," in *Culture, Communication, and Dependency: The Tradition of H. A. Innis*, ed. William Melody, Liora Salter, and Paul Heyer (Norwood, N.J.: Ablex, 1981).

38. Innis, *Cod Fisheries*, 2.

39. Innis, *Cod Fisheries*, 11.

40. Harold A. Innis et al., *The Diary of Simeon Perkins*, 5 vols. (Westport, Conn.: Greenwood, 1969–1978).

41. S. D. Clark, "The Contribution of H. A. Innis to Canadian Scholarship," in *Culture, Communication, and Dependency: The Tradition of H. A. Innis*, ed. William Melody, Liora Salter, and Paul Heyer (Norwood, N.J.: Ablex, 1981), 27–28.

42. William Westfall, "The Ambivalent Verdict: Harold Innis and Canadian History," in *Culture, Communication, and Dependency: The Tradition of H. A. Innis*, ed. William Melody, Liora Salter, and Paul Heyer (Norwood, N.J.: Ablex, 1981).

43. Harold A. Innis, *The Bias of Communication* (1951; reprint, with an introduction by Paul Heyer and David Crowley, Toronto: University of Toronto Press, 1995), 190.

44. For example, see Ian Parker, "Innis, Marx, and the Economics of Communication," in *Culture, Communication, and Dependency: The Tradition of H. A. Innis*, ed. William Melody, Liora Salter, and Paul Heyer (Norwood, N.J.: Ablex, 1981).

45. For example, see Daniel Drache, ed., *Staples, Markets, and Cultural Change: Harold Innis* (Montreal: McGill-Queen's University Press, 1995); William Melody, Liora Salter, and Paul Heyer, eds., *Culture Communication and Dependency: The Tradition of H. A. Innis* (Norwood, N.J.: Ablex, 1981); Robin Neill, *A New Theory of Value: The Canadian Economics of H. A. Innis* (Toronto: University of Toronto Press, 1972).

Chapter Three

Political Economy Inspires
Communication Studies

It has seemed to me that the subject of communication offers possibilities.

—Harold A. Innis

Another world war. Innis had experienced the first from inside the horrifying crucible of battle. He payed the price with a shattered leg that took almost six years to heal, but the mental trauma he suffered at the battle of Vimy Ridge would linger until the end. He was wiser now and observed the current vortex in Europe from outside rather than within. Enlisting in any capacity was, of course, out of the question. Yet, he was also distrustful, even disdainful, of those politicians and civilians who administered to the cause on the home front, "After eight months of the mud and lice and rats of France, in which much of the time was spent cursing government officials in Ottawa, I have without doubt developed an abnormal slant. I have never had the slightest interest since that time in people who were helping in the war with a job in Ottawa or in London."[1] Harsh words, especially since a number of his colleagues were headed in that direction.

He remained with the university and defended the ideals the war was ostensibly fighting to preserve. Innis felt it imperative that the university maintain its standards and curriculum, or, to use a more recent phrase that became ubiquitous in the aftermath of September 11, 2001, "they will win." He does not equivocate, "The social scientist will do well, and cannot do better than, to follow the advice of his masters and specialize in his own interests. In other words he can make his most effective contribution to the maintenance of morale on the home front, to the advancement of his interests, and to the solution of the problems of democracy by showing confidence in the traditions of his subject and by minding his own business. He must either do this or throw in his hand to the enemy."[2]

Needless to say, this attitude put him at odds with colleagues and bureaucrats. But he stuck to his principled guns, published *The Cod Fisheries: The History of an International Economy,*[3] and traveled to California in 1941 to lecture and to Quebec in 1943 for a brief vacation.

He also began to move in a new direction. If the study of staples led him to touch on the importance of transportation and communication, the study of one of those staples, pulp and paper, opened a door to the newly emergent field of communication studies. He simply followed pulp and paper through its subsequent stages: newspapers and journalism, books, and advertising. In other words, from looking at a natural resource–based industry he turned his attention to a cultural industry in which information, and ultimately knowledge, was a commodity that circulated, had value, and empowered those who controlled it. He began by taking a series of voluminous notes that eventually comprised his as yet unpublished "History of Communications" manuscript (see appendix A). Innis eventually published his ideas on the economic and cultural aspects of three centuries of the printed word, and then went beyond this interest by looking at other media in the context of history writ large. For the moment, however, he was content to gather the requisite materials and to maintain his status as the doyen of Canadian economic history.

Part of his persona as an economic historian entailed committee and editorial work. In 1941, he helped found the Economic History Association and its signature publication, the *Journal of Economic History.* Although the association and journal were American based, Innis had strong ties to the Chicago milieu out of which they sprang. Several years before his death, he was appointed president of the association. These ventures were sustained by pillars of scholarly support that were much harder to come by in Canada. Philanthropy, along the lines of what John D. Rockefeller, Andrew Carnegie, and so on had made available to American-based research, was scarce. Innis knew that government assistance was needed. He therefore took an active role in founding the Canadian Social Science Research Council in 1940, and its sibling organization, the Humanities Research Council of Canada, in 1944. Today, these organizations exist in combination as the Social Science and Humanities Research Council of Canada, which provides patronage to a wide range of scholarly activities.

Beginning in 1943, the more Innis sought to solidify support for academic research in Canada, the more he heard a siren call from the United States. Not surprisingly, it came from the University of Chicago. With the retirement of Chester W. Wright, who had been his doctoral supervisor, the Department of Economics sought a replacement. Innis's pedigree and accomplishments rendered him the number one candidate—in fact, accounts of the way he was courted leave the impression that it would settle for no one but Innis. He traveled to Chicago to discuss the offer. Whatever he hinted at that he might want was his to command. He weighed the pros and cons and decided that his Canadian roots ran too deep to transplant. Besides, the war was still on and the eventual necessity of dealing with its aftermath in Canada was a task that could not be shirked.

Chicago's response to his rejection of its offer was far from defeatist. It said, in effect, that the door would still be open over the next few years should he decide to reconsider. One can only speculate about a parallel universe where Innis relocates to Chicago to spend the remainder of his years working there on his communications project. Most certainly, publishing out of the United States would have made a difference by attracting an audience more quickly and continuing the tradition of the Chicago School; perhaps it would have even influenced the course of American media studies by providing a challenge to the dominant paradigm of effects research. As it was, he published *Empire and Communications* in 1950 with Oxford in England, and his unconventional historiography was almost completely ignored.[4] *The Bias of Communication* was released in 1951 under the auspices of his own university's press.[5] It found little acceptance, even in Canada, where he was still viewed as the Innis of the fur trade and cod fisheries—until the 1960s when Marshall McLuhan exhorted his readers to take seriously the writings on media done by his former University of Toronto colleague.

With the Chicago offer now out of sight, but perhaps not out of mind, Innis immersed himself in administrative labors. Without a doubt, this must have curtailed the amount of time he could put into his scholarly projects. Not only was he the head of his department, he was consulted on the establishment of an institute of business administration, asked to help explore the possibility of the university creating a school of journalism, and made chairman of a committee to assess and propose a restructuring of the School of Graduate Studies. He had become, in effect, one of the most influential academics, not only at the University of Toronto, but also nationally, as attested to by the honorary degree bequeathed to him by the University of New Brunswick in 1944. There is a small irony here, given that he would later criticize the practice of universities awarding such degrees because he felt that they were too often given to undeserving candidates.

Today, it is Innis's published writings that are the source of his influence. In his own time this was not always so. The eminent classicist Eric Havelock, in a memoir reflecting on his years at the University of Toronto (1929–1947) and his collegial relations with Innis, sees his colleague in ways that question the dedicated scholar point of view conveyed in the authorized biography of Innis by Donald Grant Creighton. While greatly admiring and respecting Innis, Havelock notes that his colleague was "ambitious" to the extent that the "[e]xercise of power and influence was something he valued, and sought, and achieved. While condemning the distractions public service might involve, to the detriment of scholarship, he readily accepted appointment to public bodies and commissions which could give him contacts with he powers that be."[6]

Havelock goes on to point out how Innis courted the favor of the president of the university and had a politically conservative public persona. He was, for Havelock at this time, not a "radical" or an "outsider," but an "insider," albeit one who did eventually become an intellectual outsider when his later communications work transcended the disciplinary norms of political economy.

It must be noted that Havelock, as a result of his left-liberal and progressive leanings, was not an "insider." He occasionally found himself on the opposite side of an issue from Innis—one of the consequences of this opposition, Havelock feels, is that when Innis was promoted, he was not. There was also an intellectual conservatism to the university that Havelock found troubling, "I can ruefully testify to this from personal experience. The doctrines not only of Marx but also of Freud were under a virtual ban in Toronto."[7] Apparently, there is no published or archival evidence to suggest that Innis ever perceived such constraints within the university. If he did, and did not challenge them, it might throw into question his numerous and insistent arguments in favor of academic freedom.

Havelock finally left the University of Toronto in 1947 and spent most of the remainder of his career at Harvard and Yale Universities. His characterization of Innis as a political conservative might come as a surprise to many left-leaning academics in Canada who have adopted Innis as a patron saint. It is, however, not completely accurate. Certainly, Innis curried administrative favor and opposed Marxism and socialism, but he also advocated social justice, was sympathetic to labor, and spoke out on behalf of marginalized regions by urging the government to take responsible measures on their behalf. One might be tempted to call him a radical conservative, or to use the term sometimes applied to him in Canada, a Red Tory. His later communications work, especially his critique of culture, confuses matters even further as he vacillates between being a populist and an elitist.

Notwithstanding Innis's opposition to socialism and Marxism on the home front, he willingly accepted an invitation from the Academy of Sciences of the Soviet Union to visit Moscow and Leningrad in June 1945. The war in Europe was over and the academy sought to celebrate its 220th anniversary by inviting distinguished scholars from abroad. He kept a diary (which has since been published) and after returning lectured on and published a journalistic account of his impressions. The trip was an eye-opening experience. It added a global and multicultural dimension to his sense of history. He also realized that Marxism might have been an effective way to facilitate the Soviet Union's adoption of modern industrial techniques.

The trip to the Soviet Union came at a major turning point in that country's standing in the eyes of the West. During the war, the North American media, seeing the Soviet Union as a crucial ally, tried to portray its struggle against Nazi aggression in a favorable light by ignoring the abuses of Joseph Stalin and downplaying the county's political ideology. Hollywood even got into the act with films such as *Mission to Moscow* (1943) and *Song of Russia* (1943), which championed the cause of the Soviet people as individuals and ignored any reference to Marxism or socialism (nevertheless, these films would come back to haunt their makers during the House Un-American Activities Committee hearings that began in 1947). After the war in Europe ended, relations between the Soviet Union and the West soon deteriorated. During his visit, Innis sensed this coming and made a plea for what we would today call détente.

In his "Reflections on Russia," he provides a brief sketch of the history of the country.[8] He notes that the Soviet Union's siege mentality must be understood in terms of its history of being invaded, from ancient times, to Napoléon Bonaparte and then Adolf Hitler. Couple this with a Marxist attempt to bind together the nation and the result is a "producer" rather than a "consumer" ethos, "[w]hereas an economy which emphasizes consumer's goods is characterized by communication industries largely dependent on advertising and by constant efforts to reach the largest number of readers or listeners, an economy emphasizing producer's goods is characterized by communication industries largely dependent on government support. As a result of this contrast a common public opinion in Russia and the West is difficult to achieve."[9]

We must, he insists, overcome these differences and find common ground from which dialogue can be established. One avenue to such an exchange is science, as evidenced in the Academy of Sciences conference that he claims he attended for this very reason. In the previous quote, we also see a connection between political economy and communication that could be helpful in understanding the modern world. He knew a fair amount about the former; studying the latter would now become an increasing priority.

Whatever direction his new research agenda would take, Chicago still wanted him to pursue it there. In the summer of 1946, he was invited to present a three-week series of lectures—twenty-eight years after his first visit there as a summer student who simply wanted to know a little bit more about economic history. Chicago now offered him the store, literally, as indicated in a correspondence from the Division of the Social Sciences, "You would be free to develop your scholarly work exactly as you choose, without any specific teaching obligations."[10] What academic could ask for more? Here was an opportunity to develop his newfound communications interest in any direction he might choose to take it. A pure scholar might have acquiesced immediately, but Innis had a multiplicity of other commitments in Canada, and they were mounting.

Earlier that year, he became a member of the Royal Commission on Adult Education serving the province of Manitoba, and before leaving for Chicago he was elected president of the Royal Society of Canada. Another factor that predisposed him to stay in Canada was the escalating Cold War and military buildup in the United States. The flirtation with Chicago ended decisively in 1947 when he was appointed dean of the University of Toronto's newly revamped graduate school.

With such diverse involvements, it seems remarkable that he was able to publish in such a prolific fashion. Yet, these administrative commitments may not have been without consequences for his writing. The last full-fledged book he authored was *Cod Fisheries* in 1940. Subsequent books, such as *Political Economy in the Modern State, Bias of Communication,* and *Changing Concepts of Time,*[11] are primarily essay collections (although some of the essays were written expressly for those texts rather than reprints), and *Empire and Communications* is derived from a lecture series. His writings, even those written prior to the notoriously opaque later efforts on communications, show little evidence of having been edited—sentences are often awkward and the prose style demands patience and knowledge on the part of the reader. Although Innis admired writers who broached similar themes and made them accessible to a wide audience, such as Lewis Mumford in the United States and Gordon Childe in England, he could not emulate them.

Political Economy in the Modern State came out just before his deanship. It is an attempt to bring together various essays written since 1933 (some were discussed in chapter 1), along with two convocation addresses, one for the University of New Brunswick, the other for his alma mater, McMaster University. There are also newer entries written just prior to or expressly for the volume. It is a pivotal book, although one not often cited by Innis commentators, in which his interest in communications can be seen emerging out of economic history. The preface is one of the most telling and compelling statements in his entire oeuvre. It serves to highlight the direction his future work will take and establishes the critical stance it will employ.

He begins by declaring that the purpose of the book is to serve as "a guide and as a warning" to servicemen returning from the war who are now finding themselves as students once again." The critically informed and outspoken views presented suggest the work of a senior scholar, sure of his stature, who is now willing to take risks. Immediately, we are confronted with Plato's passage in *Phaedrus* where Socrates imparts a cautionary lesson about the invention of writing, noting that it will attenuate memory, "create forgetfulness in the learner's souls," and give not truth "but the semblance of truth," which will make its users "appear to be omniscient," but to "generally know nothing" by having the "show of wisdom without the reality." Innis then segues this twenty-five-hundred-year-old media critique into a lesson for recent modernity:

> Since this was written the printing press and the radio have enormously increased the difficulties of thought. . . . Freedom of the press and freedom of speech have been possible largely because they have permitted the production of words on an unprecedented scale and made them powerless. Oral and written words have been harnessed to the demands of modern industrialism and in advertising have been made to find new markets for goods. Each new invention which enhances their power in that direction weakens their power in other directions.[12]

He goes on to warn of the dangers of specialization in the social sciences. Political economy, the discipline in the title of the book, is for him only a convenience, "The most important thing to be said about this term is that it is not important," and follows with, "It is the essence of the philosophy of the social sciences that concern should be given primarily to their limitations."[13] This attitude might possibly be explained with reference to an intellectual corner he was now turning. The traditional humanities were becoming increasingly important: who would have thought that the hard-nosed economist of staples such as fur, lumber, and fish, would open his next book by citing Plato? Another factor behind what amounts to a plea for interdisciplinarity is his increasing recognition of the role of media in mediating economic relations, "The compilation and dissemination of information as to prices has been dependent on the effectiveness of communication in the newspapers, the radio and other media."[14] He calls for "the necessity of perspective," which seems to suggest an integrative and global approach that can discern broad historical patterns and processes—he favorably cites Oswald Spengler, Alfred Kroeber, and Arnold Toynbee as exemplars, and they significantly influenced his soon-to-be-realized conception of the history of communications.

He laments the decline of culture, blames nationalism and religion, and then decries Canadian publishing's dependence on the United States and Britain. Although Innis is frequently seen today as a quintessential Canadian nationalist and does declare it as his "bias," what he seems to be advocating is a cultural nationalism from within, not one that is legislated for by government mandate, and especially not one that derives from programs drafted by social scientists.

These clarion calls in the preface to *Political Economy in the Modern State* are an avowed attempt "to interrelate patterns of Canadian development with those of the Western World in the realization that much remains to be done before the outlines and the details of the pattern can be clearly discerned."[15] Despite this statement, the book—which opens with an essay on the economic history of the newspaper and ends with the one on the Soviet Union just discussed—contains far more about the Western world than it does about Canada, thereby setting the tone for the research that preoccupied him until his death six years later.

The opening essay, "The Newspaper in Economic Development," is a major foray into the field now known as the history of communications or media history. Innis looks at three centuries in the evolution of the press in thirty-four pages. It could have been a three-hundred-page book if all the revealing connections were fully contextualized and extended to completion, as he had done earlier with fur and fish. However, the newspaper was only one of a number of media he wanted to explore, so the approach is very much slash and burn. Nevertheless, the swath he cuts through the subject presents it in a new light. He was aware that previous histories covered similar ground, but they had emphasized the political influence of the press in history, especially regarding issues pertaining to the presence or absence of a free press.

Other aspects of the medium interest him, particularly the power of advertising, which actually increased with the rise of the penny press in the first half of the nineteenth century. Although the penny papers removed ads from the front page and replaced them with news, advertising became increasingly important, helped keep the cost of the papers down, and expanded the range of goods and services that attracted consumers. Of the penny press itself, we learn of its general influence, not its origins—there is, for example, no mention of the first penny paper, the *New York Sun* (1833), although he does mention the first British entry, the *Daily Telegraph* (1855). Regardless, the essay espouses other priorities, such as the advent of the steam-driven press and the importance of the telegraph (and later the submarine cable) in making available a greater supply of news and giving rise to news agencies such as the Associated Press.

Not surprisingly, given his experiences in World War I, he notes how, beginning with the American Civil War (actually the Crimean War, which he does not mention), the marriage of telegraphy and journalism not only speeded up the demand for news from increasingly greater distances, but it also yielded a condensed style of exposition accessible to a wider readership than ever before. His own prose style being far from journalistic, Innis laments the restrictions on language that sprang from this new journalism. These shifts, including the use of bold headlines, accelerated with the rivalry between and Joseph Pulitzer and William Randolf Hearst that began shortly before the turn of the twentieth century. Innis, however, does not employ the term normally used to describe what resulted, yellow journalism—doubtlessly he would have been fascinated by a film such as Orson Welles' *Citizen Kane* (1941), which dramatizes this period.

During the early twentieth century, he notes the significance of the rise of tabloids. The New York *Daily News* in 1919 and Hearst's New York *Mirror* in

1924 receive commentary. He notes that at this time even "[d]epartment store advertising became news" and the newspaper declined as a political force.[16] There are numerous and impressive other details of press history embedded in his cryptic prose, including a brief passage on the role of the radio, where he notes how it became an effective vehicle for dictators. This is a notion Marshall McLuhan would explore at greater length in his *Understanding Media: The Extensions of Man.*[17]

The second essay in *Political Economy in the Modern State,* "An Economic Approach to English Literature in the Nineteenth Century," logically follows themes explored in the first. It gives part of the book at least the semblance of being a continuous narrative authored for the occasion rather than an essay compendium. Innis employs an avowedly social evolutionary point of view, favorably citing both Leslie Stephens and Herbert Spencer, but understandably preferring the more literary variant of that paradigm espoused by the former. The nineteenth century is seen as a transition period from the rationalism of eighteenth-century Enlightenment to the irrationalism of the twentieth century resulting from the proliferation of advertising and mass propaganda. His overview considers fiction and nonfiction books as well as periodicals, along with a brief assessment of the readership drawn to these publications.

Technological and contextual factors, rather than an ideational zeitgeist, underscore but do not determine (he was at this time and would very much remain a humanist) the shifts in literatures and their audiences the essay explores. Something as seemingly mundane as paper is seen as crucial. In the first half of the twentieth century, its availability gradually increased with the development of more efficient processes for the manufacture of rag paper. Then, during the last three decades the advent of paper made from wood pulp decreased the medium's cost to an even greater degree, further escalating book and periodical production. The technical means though which printed material was replicated also saw significant innovations, such as the steam press, the rotary press, and the linotype machine. Illustrations were also a major part of book and periodical publishing during this period. Woodcut engravings, although time consuming to prepare, occurred in greater numbers throughout the century, eventually being displaced in the last two decades by the halftone process for reproducing photographs.

Many authors and publications are cited. Charles Dickens, for example, began as a journalist and a journalistic quality is said to inflect his works, which attained a massive readership as the price of novels dropped in the second half of the nineteenth century. The universities, Oxford, Cambridge, and London after its inception in 1827, became training grounds for nonfiction writers. This was especially noticeable in the sciences. Writers were now able to disseminate their ideas through a wider variety of book publishing options, professional journals, and general interest periodicals. Once again, these observations suggest the framework for a major book-length study, but Innis sees them only as part of a wider historical project integrating political economy and communications.

Although most of the remainder of *Political Economy in the Modern State* is given over to reprinting essays that go back a decade, two more recent efforts make up what amounts to the centerpiece of the volume: "On the Economic Significance of Cultural Factors" and the title essay "Political Economy in the Modern State." The writing here involves as many twists and connections as anything we find in *Bias of Communication*. Innis is clearly, or to be more accurate, unclearly, delineating a rationale for where he is headed, "We need a sociology or a philosophy of the social sciences and particularly economics, an economic history of knowledge, or an economic history of economic history."[18] In both these essays, social and intellectual history are conflated into something resembling a free associationist sociology of knowledge.

The two essays also comment on everything from the alphabet as contrasted with Chinese writing, to the history of literature, Puritanism, democracy, and the state of the university. There are, and this trend would characterize his later writings as a whole, an abnormally large number of citations from memoirs, letters, and biographies—examples of history viewed from the inside, as it were, being used as source material for someone whose sweeping approach to the subject emphasized pattern and process rather than individual contributions. These essays also see civilization in a state of near collapse as a result of the triumph of irrationalism, consumerism, and the aftermath of two world wars. His characterization of the nineteenth century as one of relative peace (perhaps he was thinking of Canada here) might irk a number of historians, especially those who have studied the United States during this period.

The critique he develops is radical. There is even a passing flirtation with Karl Marx, who "showed awareness of pressure groups and emphasized the importance of the study of technology and the means of production," which for Innis can inform the way technological change impacts "on economic and political institutions."[19] Far more subversive, given the milieu in which he worked, is the following, "In a sense religion is an effort to organize irrationality and as such appears in all large-scale organizations of knowledge."[20] There seems to be a kinship here, perhaps unsuspected, with Marx's famous "religion is the opium of the people" observation, where he sees it serving the interests of the dominant ideology. It might also be supposed that by seeing religion as organized irrationalism, comparisons with Sigmund Freud might be relevant. Innis, however, was completely dismissive of Freud, seeing him as a manifestation of twentieth-century irrationalism rather than one of its major diagnosticians.

As an agnostic who favorably cites Marx and questions the role of religion in modernity, Innis would certainly have raised eyebrows at the University of Toronto or virtually any other academic institution in Canada at this time. And indeed, many eyebrows were raised, but most of them quickly became furrowed as he gnomically leapt to his next—and usually—less controversial point. He knew that sustained, point-of-view arguments would make him a ready target. Therefore, like an intellectual guerrilla, he kept his critique illusive and avoided any head on confrontation that might have impeded his intellectual voice.

In a rare moment of candor and clarity, he explained his dilemma in the 1947 address "The Church in Canada," given in to a most unusual audience: board members of the United Church of Canada.[21] Without revealing his lapse of faith, or even implying he is an agnostic, he gives a respectful critique of the church for its failure to be sufficiently self-critical and for losing touch with "ideas" by putting too much energy into social activism. He prefaces this assessment with a confession that he seems to hope will temper any negative response these observations might provoke on the part of his audience. Noting that he is normally reluctant to make public speeches, an exception will be made in this case because he believes he is addressing an audience who might understand the situation whereby his department

> [i]s under constant surveillance by a wide range of individuals. If in the course of an article I make reference to a large government department or a large business organization, I will receive in an incredibly short time . . . a personal letter from the public relations officer . . . or indirectly from the president or head of the organization, explaining that my remarks [are] liable to misinterpretation and inferring that the head of such an influential department in a large university should be very careful about the way in which his views are expressed. . . . For these reasons I am largely compelled to avoid making speeches in public and to resort to the careful preparation of material to be made available in print. *In most case this involves writing in such a guarded fashion that no one can understand what is written* or using quotations from the writings of authors who stand in great repute.[22]

This partly explains his stylistic elusiveness in the immediate postwar years. However, as we shall see when looking at *Bias of Communication,* some of the essays on media history, hardly controversial fare, are far more stylistically torturous than those that deal with cultural criticism.

NOTES

1. Donald Grant Creighton, *Harold Adams Innis: Portrait of a Scholar* (1957; reprint, Toronto: University of Toronto Press, 1978), 107.

2. Creighton, *Harold Adams Innis*, 110.

3. Harold A. Innis, *The Cod Fisheries: The History of an International Economy* (1940; reprint, Toronto: University of Toronto Press, 1954).

4. Harold A. Innis, *Empire and Communications* (1950; reprint, with a foreword by Marshall McLuhan, Toronto: University of Toronto Press, 1975). Note that this book was copublished with the Oxford University Press.

5. Harold A. Innis, *The Bias of Communication* (1951; reprint, with an introduction by Paul Heyer and David Crowley, Toronto: University of Toronto Press, 1995).

6. Eric Havelock, *Harold A. Innis: A Memoir* (Toronto: The Harold Innis Foundation, 1982), 24.

7. Havelock, *Harold A. Innis*, 24.

8. Harold A. Innis, *Political Economy in the Modern State* (Toronto: University of Toronto Press, 1946).

9. Innis, *Political Economy in the Modern State*, 259.

10. Quoted in Creighton, *Harold Adams Innis*, 124.

11. Harold A. Innis, *Changing Concepts of Time* (1952; reprint, with a foreword by James W. Carey, Boulder, Colo.: Rowman & Littlefield, 2003).

12. Innis, *Political Economy in the Modern State*, vii.

13. Innis, *Political Economy in the Modern State*, viii.

14. Innis, *Political Economy in the Modern State*, ix.

15. Innis, *Political Economy in the Modern State*, xvi.

16. Innis, *Political Economy in the Modern State*, 25.

17. Marshall McLuhan, *Understanding Media: The Extensions of Man* (New York: Signet, 1964).

18. Innis, *Political Economy in the Modern State*, 46.

19. Innis, *Political Economy in the Modern State*, 86.

20. Innis, *Political Economy in the Modern State*, 98.

21. Reprinted in Harold A. Innis, *Essays in Canadian Economic History*, ed. Mary Q. Innis (Toronto: University of Toronto Press, 1962); Daniel Drache, ed., *Staples, Markets, and Cultural Change: Harold Innis* (Montreal: McGill-Queen's University Press, 1995).

22. Innis, *Essays in Canadian Economic History*, 387, emphasis added.

Chapter Four

The "History of Communications" Project

I shall attempt to outline the significance of communication in a small number of empires as a means of understanding its role in a general sense.

—Harold A. Innis

During the postwar years, Innis's "History of Communications" manuscript became a major scholarly repository. He was constantly both adding to it and drawing from it—especially when writing about the history of paper, printing, and the book. Whether this manuscript will ever be published in whole or in part is still uncertain.[1] Along with it he also complied an idea file that, thanks to the efforts of William Christian as editor, has been selectively published as the *Idea File of Harold Adams Innis.*[2] It reveals a glimpse of Innis's mind in process, and, as Christian wryly notes, "is no more opaque than most of the material Innis himself published."[3] Innis compiled this idea file during the last seven years of his life. In it we can see a wealth of concepts and connections—for which "History of Communications" provides the broad database—that would be woven into the kaleidoscopic tapestry of his later writings on media history.

Another factor influencing Innis's turn toward communications was the influence of classical scholarship.[4] The classics department at the University of Toronto was one of the most prominent in North America. Innis might never have pursued this line of inquiry were it not for the collegial presence of leading figures in the field, such as Charles Norris Cochrane, Edward Thomas Owen, and Eric Havelock. Cochrane was especially influential. Hailing from Protestant, rural Ontario and a graduate of the University of Toronto, he also served in the army during World War I. His *Christianity and Classical Culture: A Study of Thought and Action from Augustus to Augustine,*[5] published a year before his death, along with his efforts to make knowledge gathered in the university more accessible, inspired Innis. The debt is acknowledged in the preface to *Empire and Communications,* "An interest in the general problem was stimulated by the late Professor C. N. Cochrane and the late Professor E. T. Owen."[6] Five years earlier, a fuller statement of his appreciation of Cochrane appeared in an obituary published in the *Canadian Journal of Economics and Political Science.*

Although Owen is also cited in *Empire and Communications,* this is perhaps more for his researches into Hellenic civilization than for his approach, which is far more literary than the one Innis espoused. Havelock's importance was due to the interdisciplinary vision he shared with Innis, which eschewed any hard-and-fast division between the humanities and the social sciences, and because of his interest in the interplay between power and knowledge in historical change. It has been argued that Havelock eventually became more indebted to Innis than vice versa and that his work is an extension of Innis's take on Greek civilization, the alphabet, and the social consequences of technological change in communication media.[7] Since Innis's death, Havelock has written extensively on these subjects—in ways that have significantly influenced Marshall McLuhan—but he has attributed the similarity between his project and Innis's to "a matter of happy coincidence."[8]

Following Innis's being appointed dean of the graduate school in 1947 came an offer from Oxford University to give a series of lectures on a subject of his choosing relevant to the economic history of the British Empire. Sponsored by the Beit Fund, these lectures were delivered the following year and were eventually published as *Empire and Communications* in 1950. Drawing from "History of Communications," plus adding to it material on ancient and classical civilizations, Innis's lectures were organized in a comparative and systematic way, with the Innisian style much in evidence. Underpinning the wide-ranging historiography of these lectures was a series of concepts relating to communication and culture that would later compel separate elaboration. They constitute the essays in *The Bias of Communication* published a year after *Empire and Communications.*[9]

One of these essays, however, "Minerva's Owl," which serves as the first chapter of *Bias of Communication,* dates from May 1947 and is worth discussing here since it sketches in broad convoluted brush strokes the historiographical approach Innis assumes in *Empire and Communications.* "Minerva's Owl" began life as Innis's presidential address to the Royal Society of Canada. It left the audience it addressed somewhat bewildered, but it has also been rightly called "the most important general statement of the last phase of Innis's career."[10]

The title of the essay recall's Georg Hegel's evocation of mythology in his *Philosophy of History.*[11] The implication—"Minerva's owl only takes flight in the gathering dusk"—is that classical civilization reached its apogee just before its fall, and only then does Minerva's owl take flight and allow for an assessment of all that had gone before. Perhaps Innis identified with the owl, since the very title of his essay and its subject matter represent his flight from political economy and conventional academe to a new and largely uncharted continent that he called the history of communications. He opens with a statement of intent that resonates like a clarion call to such a degree it has been selected as the epigraph for this book, "I have attempted to suggest that Western civilization has been profoundly influenced by communication and that marked changes in communications have had important implications."[12]

Here, he uses the term "communication," which generally refers to a process or an activity whereby messages are produced, transmitted, and interpreted, to signify both the process—different languages and various forms of writing—and the medium through which it takes place—oral speech, stone, clay, papyrus, parchment, printed paper, and so on. For the first of the three books to follow, *Empire and Communications* (*Changing Concepts of Time*[13] was the third), Innis added an "s" to its key term. This suggests greater inclusiveness, or as a recent textbook on the subject puts it, communication + medium = communications.[14]

"Minerva's Owl" promises both more and less than it delivers. It opens with the avowed intent of tracing the "implications of the media of communication for the character of knowledge and to suggest that a monopoly or an oligopoly of knowledge is built up to the point that equilibrium is disturbed."[15] Innis declares that he will start with ancient Mesopotamia and conclude with a look at cinema and radio. However, he barely touches the twentieth century. The essay is a baffling read of insightful observations followed by statements that seem to bear no logical connection to what preceded them; more often than not, they lead in a completely new direction rather than resolve what has gone before. It is hard not to imagine bewilderment on the part of the audience when the paper was first read, especially since Innis was not deemed an especially charismatic speaker.

That said, if the essay is read for its insights and without regard to any expectation of expository continuity, it offers a wealth of thought-provoking observations unified through a series of media-related historical examples. In the beginning, which for Innis means Mesopotamia, their was clay, the reed stylus used to write on it, and the wedge-shaped cuneiform script. Thus did civilization arise, along with an elite group of scribe priests who eventually codified laws. Egypt followed suit, using papyrus, the brush, and hieroglyphic writing. The Greeks took a different turn, breaking with the elaborate forms of script used in earlier empires. They appropriated the Phoenician alphabet and modified it into a flexible system of communication that initially worked hand in hand with the earlier oral tradition. Innis notes that initially in Greece the limitations of this alphabet were acknowledged—thus recalling Plato's critique of writing cited in the preface to *Political Economy and the Modern State*—but eventually the "energies in mastering the technique of writing left little possibility for considering implications of technique."[16]

Greek literacy eventually yielded restrictive laws and its civilization went into decline. (The Greek example is the most extensively discussed in the essay, no doubt as a result of the presence at the University of Toronto the aforementioned tradition of classical scholarship.) Rome rose in its stead and the administrative potential of papyrus, already evident in Egypt, was more fully realized when employing an alphabetic script. The result was an expansionist empire. He does not discuss the collapse of Rome but quickly skips to the invention of paper-and-block printing in China, the rise of vernacular literacy in the Middle Ages, and the printing revolution. Paper, printing, and the newspaper are traced through their first several centuries by abstracting part of the analysis he made in the first two essays in *Political Economy in the Modern State*. The essay ends with several cautionary observations on the implications of industrialism and mechanization that suggest the influence of Thorstein Veblen.

"Minerva's Owl" is thus a cornucopia of themes—what McLuhan would later call with respect to his own work "probes." Some of them had been touched on in earlier publications; most received fuller elaboration in the writings Innis produced during the five years that remained to him. A recurring element in the essay is the metaphoric visit of the owl itself to the various civilizations discussed, where, after finding "a resting place only at brief intervals,"[17] it flies away when they begin their decline.

How indebted to Hegel is Innis's concept of what "Minerva's Owl" represents? Certainly, both see history as a cyclical process of rise and fall, growth and decay. But the inevitability of this movement for Hegel is teleological, that is, it has a purpose, which is the progress of what he calls "Spirit" through history. As each civilization is superceded, or negated dialectically, by the one that follows it, greater enlightenment, perfection, and freedom (Spirit) is attained. Innis might follow the flight of the owl and subscribe to history as a cyclical process, but he would never see it as teleological or concede that progress is its product.

Fortunately, Innis's personality was not as distant as his writing. For those students who could weather his less-than-engaging lectures and glimpse the substance and innovative thought they embodied, he became a trusted mentor. He also held court to an endless stream of "[p]oliticians, civil servants, journalists, manufacturers, labour leaders, farmers prospectors, and scholars of all disciplines and ages."[18] The trip to England to present the Beit Lectures must have been a welcome change of routine, although he was busy revising them throughout. Side visits to Nottingham, London, Cambridge, and Paris were also on the agenda. Nevertheless, he must have experienced some anxiety given that the economic history of the British Empire—what the Beit sponsorship mandated the lectures cover—held little interest for him by this time. Instead, audiences received a comparative perspective on the history of communications in the form of six broadly cast lectures.

After his return to Toronto, he began preparing the material for publication as a book. Disruptions of his academic routine were constant. One was massive. He was invited to become a member of the Royal Commission on Transportation. It was an offer he could not refuse, given his academic expertise and concern for issues involving social policy. The appointment necessitated transcontinental travel by rail and later shunting back and forth between Ottawa and Toronto—Toronto for the weekends where one of his obligations was to give two Saturday lectures. Understandably exhausted, and occasionally ill, he still managed to see *Empire and Communications* through to publication.

Although based on lectures, *Empire and Communications* evidences the structural form and detailed analysis that one would expect from a major text dealing with comparative history. Following the introduction, there are chapters on Egypt, Babylonia, the oral tradition and Greece, the written tradition and Rome, the role of parchment and paper in the Middle Ages, and the early history of print media. Perhaps because the book is based on a series of lectures the writing is more accessible than Innis's other media-related essays. This is not to imply that *Empire and Communications* is an easy read—the many references and intellectual range can challenge even the informed reader. Yet here, more than in any of his other books, the reader is given a helpful assist into the main body of the work by means of a cogent nine-page introduction. Students who wish to explore any aspect of Innis's communications writings could do no better than to start with this introduction.

It begins with a nod to the works of Oswald Spengler, Arnold Toynbee, Alfred Kroeber, and Pitirim Sorokin, who have all studied issues pertaining to the rise and fall of civilizations, with implied lessons for the future (in the preface, George Mead, Karl Marx, Gaetano Mosca, Vilfredo Pareto, and Veblen are added to the list, which is cast in alphabetical order). The link between the supposed subject of the original lectures—the economic history of the British Empire—and what Innis will actually undertake is drawn in a loose fashion. He notes that the successes and failures of civilization writ large can inform an understanding of the British Empire, past and present. He also seems to be trying to offset possible criticism of the liberties he is taking with the theme of the Beit Lectures by arguing that an "[o]bsession with economic considerations illustrates the dangers of monopolies of knowledge and suggests the necessity of appraising its limitations."[19] The path to such a critique for him necessitates considering "the subject of communication," which he confesses as his "bias" and which he explicitly states is an outgrowth of his earlier work in political economy—he cites the railway, fur trade, and staples research, adding that he also believes the study of pulp and paper can tell us much about the history of the British Empire.

Innis sees the history of civilizations in terms of centripetal and centrifugal forces; in other words, those that aggregate and those that disperse the power they have over societies in their purview. Rome employed paper to exert centralized control across its empire by imposing a unified political and legal apparatus and is an example of the former, whereas in using parchment the medieval Catholic Church oversaw the less centralized Holy Roman Empire. This distinction, which he explores more fully in *Bias of Communication,* conforms to the time-bias or space-bias of the dominant medium employed. Time-biased media, such as stone, clay, and parchment, are durable and favor decentralized, hierarchical societies governed by a ruling theocracy. Spaced-biased media, such as papyrus and paper, favor expansionist empires that are less hierarchical and theocratic and are maintained through the administrative efficacy of these portable and inexpensive media.

The history of the West is divided into a writing and a printing period. Before the specter of technological determinism would hover over Innis, he dismisses the potential accusation in a decisive and bizarre way. He notes that "it would be presumptuous to suggest that the written or printed word has determined the course of civilizations," and follows this statement with a footnote citing Adolf Hitler's observation in *Mein Kampf* (Innis quotes the text verbatim) that throughout history it has always been the spoken, not the written word, that has brought about major political and religious changes.[20] Hitler, himself, went on to become a terrifying illustration of his own hypothesis and this is addressed later in the text:

> Governmental influence over the press was extended to radio. The loud speaker had a decisive significance for the election of the Nazis. Regions dominated by the German language responded to the appeal of the spoken word inviting them to join a larger German Reich. The Second World War became to an important extent the result of a clash between the newspaper and the radio . . . and precipitated an outbreak of savagery paralleling that of printing and the religious wars of the seventeenth century, and again devastating the regions of Germany.[21]

Part of this observation is cited by McLuhan in his foreword to *Empire and Communications.* His discussion of Hitler and radio in *Understanding Media: The Extensions of Man* seems to be an amplification of these views.[22]

Of the history of writing per se, Innis notes that much has been written, but it has been limited to narrow fields or broad generalizations. Largely but not wholly true, as we will see shortly. He follows Carl Becker in noting that writing provided "a transpersonal memory" that allows us to range beyond the world of the concrete by expanding on the possibilities inherent in using symbolic concepts. According to Innis, "Writing enormously enhanced a capacity for abstract thinking which had been evident in the growth of language in the oral tradition. . . . The old magic was transformed into a new and more potent record of the written word. Priests and scribes integrated a slowly changing tradition and provided a justification for established authority."[23] Note again his avoidance of a deterministic slant. Writing itself did not cause these changes, rather it extended and amplified what was already existent in the realm of orality.

Although the world's first civilizations emerged in Mesopotamia, in the ancient land of Sumer, Innis elects to begin his discussion with Egypt. The Nile and its periodic flooding provided the foundation in nature on which Egyptian civilization arose. Knowledge of the river's cycle was embodied in a calendar. Power followed this knowledge of time. Words were given permanency through hieroglyphics and divine kingship ruled the land. Edicts were etched in stone, literally. After 2000 B.C., absolute authority became less absolute as papyrus supplanted stone as the dominant medium for written communication. He assesses the nature of this medium, from its origins as a riverine marsh plant, to the process that prepared it to be a scroll suitable for script (Innis's description of this transformation recalls passages on the beaver and codfish in his earlier books). With the coming of papyrus, writing itself changed and assumed the more cursive form known as hieratic. The consequences were profound, "A marked increase in writing by hand was accompanied by a secularization of writing, thought, and activity. The social revolution between the Old and New Kingdom was marked by a flow of eloquence and a displacement of religious by secular literature."[24]

This shift brought forth an army of scribes who became a privileged class in an increasingly democratic but still hierarchical society. Using Alexander Moret and Gordon Childe as sources, Innis describes this process, but he puts much more emphasis than they do on the ramifications inherent in the medium used to write and the form of script that was employed. Egyptian communications, for Innis, was never able to shed completely its hieroglyphic origins. This created a scenario whereby the "limitations of the Egyptian empire were in part the result of the inflexibility of religious institutions supported by a monopoly over a complex system of writing."[25] However, writing with an abundant medium such as papyrus (as opposed to stone) did enable Egypt to make important discoveries in science—especially in astronomy with respect to the development of a more efficient calendrical system—and medicine.

The short suggestive chapter on Egypt leaves numerous points unresolved.

It is succeeded by a more lengthy one, which although labeled "Babylonia," actually deals with the entire Mesopotamian region over three millennia. Once again, nature provides both a foundation for the societies in question and a point of departure for Innis's analysis. The Tigris and Euphrates Rivers were crucial to the city-states that formed in the region, not as a result of a cycle of ebb and flood as was the case with the Nile in Egypt, but because dependency on these rivers necessitated an organization of labor to harness them through irrigation. Coincidentally, just as the Nile supplied papyrus as a medium for written communication in Egypt, so the rivers in southern Mesopotamia yielded the alluvial clay that Sumerian civilization rendered into writing tablets and building bricks. Innis describes the process whereby a reed stylus was used to incise, in wet clay, pictographs (picture writing) and ideograms (conventionalized abstract signs). Eventually, a more streamlined system of writing emerged that involved the wedge-shaped script known as cuneiform.

> These clay tablets could be rendered permanent by firing them: Indestructibility insured inviolability for commercial and personal correspondence. Though admirably adapted by its durability for use over a long period of time, clay as a heavy material was less suited as a medium of communication over larger areas. Its general character favored the collection of permanent records in widely scattered communities. . . . The characteristics of clay favoured the conventionalization of writing, decentralization of cities, the growth continuing organization in the temples, and religious control.[26]

He then describes the social formations that resulted, along with the warfare between rival city-states that led to the Babylonians under Hammurabi creating a "territorial state" with unified laws, a common capital, and a standardized calendar. Mathematics (especially pertaining to weights and measures) and time reckoning flourished, along with a sexigesimel system of numeration (based on units of sixty) that survives to the present day.

The history of the region is examined further by looking at trade and warfare. It underwent a media revolution of sorts when in the middle of the second millennium B.C. the Phoenicians invented a prototype of the alphabet that used twenty-two consonantal characters. Innis's assessment of the context in which this occurred still holds up in light of recent research.[27] He notes that "[t]he Phoenicians had no monopoly of knowledge in which religion and literature might hamper the development of writing. The necessities of an expanding maritime trade demanded a swift and concise method of recording transactions and the use of a single shortened script . . . commerce and the alphabet were inextricably interwoven, particularly when letters of the alphabet were used as Numerals. Phoenician cities, rather than capitals of empires, reflected a concern with trade."[28] He then notes how such a system of writing, especially when it passed to the Hebrews, resulted in reverence for the word, monotheism, and a disinterest in the kind of architecture and imagery that were so prominent in Egypt and Babylonia.

The Phoenician alphabet eventually traveled to Greece, where, after several modifications, most notably the adding of vowels, it had far-reaching implications. Innis seems more comfortable discussing communication and culture in ancient Greece than he is when dealing with the Near Eastern civilizations; no doubt the tradition of classical scholarship at the University of Toronto had over the years bequeathed to him a Hellenic expertise, whereas he seems to have studied Egypt and Babylonia more recently on his own and without the benefit of collegial expertise. Understanding the history of communications in Greece following the introduction of the alphabet meant understanding the clash between a primary oral culture under assault from the written word. In laying the ground rules for this undertaking, he requotes and reelaborates on the passage from Plato's *Phaedrus* that is part of the preface to *Political Economy in the Modern State.*

He assesses Aristotle as a major benchmark in the ascendency of the written tradition over the spoken word and in the triumph of prose over poetry. Yet, as Innis is quick to point out, the legacy of the Greek oral tradition has not disappeared altogether. It hovers on the periphery of the history of western literate civilization and is a tradition he feels should be constantly revived. Among Greek orality's finest achievements are the Homeric epics, which he looks at (through a bias he willingly concedes is imposed by a literate transcription) in terms of the social conditions that produced them as well as with respect to the linguistic devices they employed.

The chapter on Greece is, in effect, an amalgam of cultural history—the rise and fall of the gods, shifts in philosophy, and the overall zeitgeist—and social history—the formation of the city-states, political and legal changes, and the strategic importance of trade. Ultimately, for Innis, writing added to the mix, not unity, but disunity and divisiveness, "The spread of writing contributed to the collapse of Greek civilization by widening the gap between city states."[29] What he is actually referring to here is the disequilibrium created, not by writing per se, but by a tyrannical and monopolistic overextension of it. Centuries earlier, the written and oral traditions had more "balance" relative to one another, "The strength of the oral tradition and the relative simplicity of the alphabet checked the possible development of a highly specialized profession of scribes and the growth of a monopoly of the priesthood over education."[30] This observation is a key to Innis's critique of culture (see chapter 5) that is based on his (some say romantic) homage to the oral tradition—his ideal is actually not a scenario of pure orality, but one where oral and literate traditions coexist, with the former monitoring the latter.

The torch of literacy that in the end contributed to the decline of Greece was transposed to Rome where it helped a new civilization arise—Innis's sense of the movement of history here is very Hegelian, in that he traces a theme, literacy in this instance, through successive stages in the realization of its possibilities. Once again, he observes how a society that was primarily oral and based on forms of reciprocity linked to kinship gave way to one where written laws and contracts became the matrix of social relationships. *Ancient Law,* Henry Sumner Maine's still revered classic, is one on Innis's major sources.[31] Following Maine, Innis traces the history of the Roman Republic through its military conquests, but he adds side trips to assess the role of the Ptolemaïs in Egypt and the great library tradition in Alexandria.

Papyrus from Egypt helped extend Roman literacy, which according to Innis, "contributed to the downfall of the Republic and the emergence of the empire."[32] One of the consequences of the empire was the establishment of libraries to rival Alexandria, not only in Rome itself (according to Innis, twenty-eight were built during the fourth century A.D.), but throughout the rest of the empire as well. He does not see this as a result of the veneration of knowledge, but citing Veblen's famous phrase, as an example of "conspicuous consumption." Slaves trained as scribes supplied the demand by mass-producing books. As a result, literacy (in Latin) became widespread, as did propaganda. Ultimately, the "written tradition dependent on papyrus and the roll supported an emphasis on centralized bureaucratic administration. Rome became dependent on the army, territorial expansion, and law at the expense of trade and an international economy."[33]

Facing internal challenges from Christianity, which used the time-biased medium of parchment (treated animal skins) and the codex (the book with facing pages), and external challenges from barbarian invaders who disdained literacy, Rome collapsed under the weight of an overextended and undermaintained empire. A more stable experiment in statecraft emerged in its stead, "The Byzantine empire developed on the basis of a compromise between organization reflecting the bias of different media: that of papyrus in the development of an imperial bureaucracy in relation to a vast area and that of parchment in the development of an ecclesiastical hierarchy in relation to time."[34]

One element relevant to Innis's subsequent assessment of the Middle Ages in the "Parchment and Paper" chapter appears near the end of his examination of the fate of the Roman Empire: How the new medium of parchment was produced. We get a brief but detailed description—again one is reminded of earlier discussions of the processes involved in preparing beaver pelts and drying cod. He then considers the new medium's communicative potential:

The parchment codex was adapted to large books in emphasizing facility of reference and consequently lent itself to religion and law in the scriptures and in the codes. A permanent medium suited to use over wide areas facilitated the establishment of libraries and the production of a limited number of large books which could be copied. . . . [A]n extensive censorship emerged in which material suited to religion and law was given enormous emphasis.[35]

He then describes the monastic tradition that spread throughout Europe following the fall of Rome and how its monopoly of knowledge was maintained through literacy and control over the production of parchment and books. His view of the Middle Ages, however, is far from Eurocentric. Consideration is given to the literate tradition of Islam (referred to as "Mohammedanism") with its veneration of the word and disdain for the kind of iconic imagery that was becoming a symbolic referent to Christianity. And, just as Christianity owed a debt to the medium of parchment, so Islam did with respect to paper. This leads him to look at the source for that medium, China, which invented it in the second century A.D., and then five hundred years later combined it with block printing to produce the world's first printed books. But China did not have an alphabet, so it developed along different lines from the West—he does point out that one advantage of the Chinese nonalphabetic script is that it could be understood throughout the empire by people speaking mutually unintelligible dialects.

Paper gradually entered western Europe through trade and was eventually manufactured there by the thirteenth century. Along with it came Arabic numerals. Both contributed to a burgeoning commercial economy and urbanization. Gradually, the Catholic Church's monopoly over literacy was challenged as paper facilitated the spread of literacy in the vernacular (the local or regional language), widening the gap between the religious and the secular, "Paper supported the growth of trade and of cities and of education beyond the control of the monasteries and, in turn, of the Church and the cathedrals. The rise of the vernacular was reflected in the patronage of literature by the courts and in the increasing role of lawyers."[36] The inherent time-bias of the Church, with its attendant monopoly of knowledge, thus collided with the space-bias of emergent nations whose bureaucratic facility was expedited (is it was in China) through the extensive use of paper.

In the final chapter, "Paper and Printing," Innis goes over some of the terrain he had covered in previous writings dealing with the newspaper, book and periodical publishing, and pulp and paper industry. What is new is his examination of the establishment of the printing press itself in the fifteenth century and its history in early modern Europe. Eventually, paper, printing, and vernacular literacy rendered the nation-state triumphant over the Catholic Church, shattering the ecclesiastical monopoly of knowledge. But new monopolies arose, he argues, whereby governments sought to censure printed material, and several examples of this practice are assessed. He concludes the book with a reminder that such constraints are still with us albeit in a more subtle guise, "In the United States the dominance of the newspaper led to large-scale development of monopolies of communication in terms of space. . . . Regional monopolies have been strengthened by monopolies of press associations."[37] These cautionary words are as apropos today as when he wrote them, perhaps more so, given the recent escalation of ownership concentration whereby single conglomerates can control both print and electronic media outlets.

Although based on lectures, *Empire and Communications* has sufficient detail in its analysis, and originality, to be regarded as a landmark book, a classic in fact. This was not the view at the time. Reviews were few and tended to range from lukewarm to negative. Those who had known Innis as the political economist of staples were perplexed by his new found indulgence in media history, a discipline or subdiscipline that was nonexistent at the time. Communication studies itself was only just emerging as a component of the university curriculum. It was more concerned with studying the effects of contemporary media by examining their content than it was in assessing, as was the case with Innis, the specific properties of the media in question or how media evolved historically. Therefore, Innis can be considered the "father" of what has become known as "medium theory," which will be discussed in conjunction with the appraisal of his legacy in chapter 5; and although he is not the first person to have studied communications history or media history, he is the first to map its contours as a discipline or subdiscipline for serious scholarly study.

Amid the minimal recognition *Empire and Communications* received when it first came out was one telling appreciation. It came from perhaps the most knowledgeable critic Innis could have had, someone whose intellectual position was in some ways similar to his own. Australian archaeologist Gordon Childe, who spent most of his academic career at the Universities of Edinburgh and London, was one of the world's leading figures in his field. He was also a popularizer, in the best sense of the term, of archaeological research, whose *Man Makes Himself* and *What Happened in History* attracted a wide nonacademic and academic readership.[38] Childe published a review of *Empire and Communications* and Innis replied.[39]

Childe saw Innis's work, despite its shortcomings, as extending an area that was glimpsed but not developed in his own. He praised the Canadian for dealing with the history of communications in terms of the media that convey information rather than through an assessment of the linguistic content of particular periods. He also seemed to sense a materialist emphasis in Innis consonant with his own Marxian-influenced approach. Nevertheless, Childe did point out several inaccuracies and misunderstandings in *Empire and Communications,* which he graciously noted were perhaps due to Innis's distance from both firsthand sources in archaeology and expert scholarly advice. He concluded the review by praising the Canadian for his courage in pursuing such an important although unconventional research area, one that had significant bearing on the archaeological work Childe and others were doing.

Innis replied by thanking Childe for the review and for being kinder than necessary. He also complimented the archaeologist for being such a lucid writer, which Innis saw as helping to break down entrenched "monopolies of knowledge." There is an obvious irony in this observation, since Innis was the opposite kind of writer and the difficulties in reading him have engendered a few interpretive monopolies of knowledge of their own, especially in Canada. Innis concluded his response by noting the importance of Childe's contribution to his own sphere of interest, a debt he had acknowledged previously in *Empire and Communications* through several citations of Childe's work.

Apparently, the two never met and both were in the twilight of their careers at the time this exchange took place. Childe, who hailed from Sydney, Australia, had espoused radical ideals early in his career. He was highly critical of both war and religion and went to Oxford while his peers were enlisting in World War I. His attitude at this time somewhat resembles Innis's during World War II, but not prior to World War I. Childe, however, leaned more to the left, flirted seriously with Marxism, and did not court the favor of university administrators or government bureaucrats. There is also an American connection and an intriguing coincidence with Innis's career. Childe taught at Berkeley during the summer of 1939, and then following World War II an attempt was made to grant him a visiting professorship at the University of Chicago. This occurred at the same time Innis was being courted by that institution. Funding problems coupled with Childe's ill health thwarted the plan. One could add, to the parallel universe scenario imagined earlier whereby Innis leaves Toronto for Chicago, the presence there of Childe, with the two colleagues inspiring one another.

Another coincidence is that the second edition of *Man Makes Himself* came out in 1951, the same year as *Bias of Communication* and a year after *Empire and Communications*. The complementarity between Childe's book and Innis's later works is significant and seems to have gone unacknowledged by Innis commentators.[40] Like Innis, Childe had a penchant for epochal historical divisions, coining widely cited terms such as "Neolithic revolution," "urban revolution" (Innis employs this term in *Empire and Communications*), and the "revolution in human knowledge." If anything, Childe is even more the materialist than Innis, putting major emphasis on economics and technology. Childe also looks at the role of writing in the ancient world and sees it as an innovation forced by productive circumstances, which profoundly influenced administration and trade. He notes how it transcended the limitations on knowledge of the oral tradition, conveyed status to its practitioners, and prompted the development of elitist class-based societies in the ancient Near East.

Although Childe's analysis very much describes what Innis called monopolies of knowledge, there is a basic difference in their historiographical approaches. Innis tends to see premodern history as comprised of fairly discrete divisions. Each epoch, whether it be defined by stone, clay, papyrus, or parchment, is assessed with respect to the way its elements interact in an extended moment in time. He is not concerned with origins or details pertaining to the transformation from one epoch to the other, but situations of before and after. An approach such as this, which looks at historical cross-sections, is sometimes called "synchronic." Childe's strategy, on the other hand, is one that could be labeled "diachronic." How a society evolves to stage A, then from A to stages B, C, and so on, is as important to him as the dynamic evidenced in each of these stages and the qualitative differences between them.

Empire and Communications, although the first full-fledged history of communications, was not the first work to explore the relationship between media and society in a broad temporal perspective. Although Innis cites numerous sources, he seems to have missed a number of intriguing precursors dating back at least three centuries. Eighteenth-century Enlightenment thinkers such as Anne-Robert-Jacques Turgot (1727–1781) and Marquis de Condorcet (1743–1794), working within the field of universal history, looked at stages in human social evolution.[41] Technology in general and the assumed progress of knowledge were the criteria on which they defined historical succession. Language, writing, and the printing press were held to be crucial elements in this panoramic unfolding, thus making at least part of their work a harbinger of the historical (but not necessarily progressive) periodization of history Innis would employ in *Empire and Communications.* Another eighteenth-century writer who shares an unacknowledged kinship with Innis is Jean-Jacques Rousseau (1712–1778). Rousseau's veneration of orality and critique of the limitations on knowledge imposed by the written word anticipates Innis's in intriguing ways.[42]

The nineteenth century saw various attempts to deal with the history of languages (through comparative philology) and the history of writing (through social evolutionism). Perhaps, the most notable effort in the latter regard is anthropologist Edward Burnet Tylor's (1832–1917) *Researches into the Early History of Mankind and the Development of Civilization,* which looks primarily at non-Western traditions.[43] As a rule, however, Innis did not draw from studies done by anthropologists. One notable exception is the work of his contemporary, Alfred Kroeber, an heir to Tylor's legacy, whose *Configurations of Culture Growth*[44] is cited as the primary influence on the essay "The Bias of Communication," in the book by the same name. Sociologists, too, are usually given little to no shrift by Innis. Karl Bücher's (1847–1930) *Industrial Evolution,* with its discussion of the history of marketing, transportation, and communication, would seem to relate directly to Innis's project, especially given the connections Bücher makes between the history of the press and political economy.[45]

During the twentieth century, some of Bücher's ideas were picked up by a figure whom many have assumed significantly influenced Innis, Chicago sociologist Robert Ezra Park (1864–1944). Park wrote on the role of the press, including several historical essays in which he dealt with its evolution as a social institution. McLuhan, as we saw in chapter 1, has made a strong but probably misguided claim that the influence of Park on Innis was profound. Yes, there are parallels, and some influence is certainly possible, but nowhere in Innis's published work do we find a citation to Park, even where we would most expect to find one: in "Paper and the Printing Press," the concluding chapter of *Empire and Communications.*

Innis followed the publication of *Empire and Communications* by wrapping up his duties with the Royal Commission on Transportation—the lengthy report was finally published in March 1951. He also gave a series of visiting lectures, most notably to the University of New Brunswick in 1950 in honor of its 150th anniversary. The lecture, "A Plea for Time," was eventually published in *Bias of Communication.* He also traveled again, to England, France, and the United States, where he was elected president of the American Economic Association. Eventually returning to his communications researches, he began imparting to them a more critical take on contemporary issues. This was exacerbated by the Korean War, which he saw as a misguided venture into American imperialism. He was equally disturbed by what he perceived as the Canadian government kowtowing to its southern Big Brother, and wrote two essays, "The Strategy of Culture" and "Military Implications of the American Constitution," that expressed his discomfort.[46]

Whether or not he knew his mortal flesh was becoming increasingly vulnerable to terminal cancer at this time is hard to say. There was a major undisclosed illness in July 1950, and before that periodic bouts of incapacitation.[47] Bedridden for most of 1952, it seems likely that the specter of serious illness had been stalking him for several years before his death and that overwork provided it with an occasional window of opportunity until it broke through with fatal consequences on November 8, 1952. In any case, a sustained writing project was now out of the question. It was all he could do to assemble the essays that would make up *Bias of Communication* and *Changing Concepts of Time* and to leave us with a legacy that continues to inspire.

NOTES

1. In addition to appendix A, see also William J. Buxton, "The Bias against Communication: On the Neglect and Non-publication of the 'Incomplete and Unrevised Manuscript' of Harold Adams Inns," *Canadian Journal of Communication* 26, nos. 2–3 (2001); Brian Shoesmith, "Introduction to Innis' 'History of Communication,'" *Continuum: The Australian Journal of Media and Culture* 7, no. 1 (1993): 121–131.

2. William Christian, ed., *The Idea File of Harold Adams Innis*, by Harold A. Innis (Toronto: University of Toronto Press, 1980).

3. Christian, *Idea File of Harold Adams Innis*, viii.

4. John Watson extensively discusses this influence and my commentary draws from his work. See John Watson, "Harold Innis and Classical Scholarship," *Journal of Canadian Studies* 12, no. 5 (1977).

5. Charles Norris Cochrane, *Christianity and Classical Culture: A Study of Thought and Action from Augustus to Augustine* (London: Oxford University Press, 1944).

6. Harold A. Innis, *Empire and Communications* (1950; reprint, with a foreword by Marshall McLuhan, Toronto: University of Toronto Press, 1975), xiii.

7. Watson believes this is the case. See Watson, "Harold Innis and Classical Scholarship."

8. Eric Havelock, *Harold A. Innis: A Memoir* (Toronto: The Harold Innis Foundation, 1982), 42.

9. Harold A. Innis, *The Bias of Communication* (1951; reprint, with an introduction by Paul Heyer and David Crowley, Toronto: University of Toronto Press, 1995).

10. Donald Grant Creighton, *Harold Adams Innis: Portrait of a Scholar* (1957; reprint, Toronto: University of Toronto Press, 1978), 127.

11. Georg Hegel, *Philosophy of History*, trans. John Sibree (1899; reprint, preface by Charles Hegel and introduction by C. J. Friedrich, New York: Dover, 1956).

12. Innis, *Bias of Communication*, 3.

13. Harold A. Innis, *Changing Concepts of Time* (1952; reprint, with a foreword by James W. Carey, Boulder, Colo.: Rowman & Littlefield, 2003).

14. David Crowley and Paul Heyer, *Communication in History: Technology, Culture, Society* (Boston: Allyn and Bacon, 2003).

15. Innis, *Bias of Communication*, 3–4.

16. Innis, *Bias of Communication*, 9; see also Harold A. Innis, *Political Economy and the Modern State* (Toronto: University of Toronto Press, 1946).

17. Innis, *Bias of Communication*, 30.

18. Creighton, *Harold Adams Innis*, 130.

19. Innis, *Empire and Communications*, 4.

20. Innis, *Empire and Communications*, 8.

21. Innis, *Empire and Communications*, 165.

22. Marshall McLuhan, *Understanding Media: The Extensions of Man* (New York: Signet, 1964).

23. Innis, *Empire and Communications*, 10.

24. Innis, *Empire and Communications*, 17.

25. Innis, *Empire and Communications*, 17.

26. Innis, *Empire and Communications*, 28.

27. For example, see Johanna Drucker, *The Alphabetic Labyrinth: Letters in History and Imagination* (London: Thames and Hudson, 1995).

28. Innis, *Empire and Communications,* 43.

29. Innis, *Empire and Communications,* 83.

30. Innis, *Empire and Communications,* 66.

31. Henry Sumner Maine, *Ancient Law: Its Connection with the Early History of Society, and Its Relation to Modern Ideas* (London: Murray, 1866).

32. Innis, *Empire and Communications,* 100.

33. Innis, *Empire and Communications,* 107.

34. Innis, *Empire and Communications,* 115.

35. Innis, *Empire and Communications,* 117.

36. Innis, *Empire and Communications,* 135–136.

37. Innis, *Empire and Communications,* 170.

38. Gordon Childe, *Man Makes Himself* (London: Watts, 1936); Gordon Childe, *What Happened in History* (Harmondsworth, UK: Penguin, 1942).

39. The review appeared in the *Canadian Journal of Economics and Political Science* 27 (February 1951). Innis replied in the next issue, *Canadian Journal of Economics and Political Science* 27 (May 1951).

40. But see Paul Heyer, "Empire, History, and Communications Viewed from the Margins: The Legacies of Gordon Childe and Harold Innis," *Continuum: The Australian Journal of Media and Culture* 7, no. 1 (1993).

41. For a fuller discussion of precursors to twentieth-century communication thought, see Paul Heyer, *Communications and History: Theories of Media, Knowledge, and Civilization* (Westport, Conn.: Greenwood, 1988).

42. Rousseau's views on writing emerged as a topic of discussion in poststructuralist thought following the publication of Jacques Derrida's *Of Grammatology,* trans. Gayatri Chakravorty Spivak (Baltimore, Md.: Johns Hopkins University Press, 1976).

43. Edward Burnet Tylor, *Researches into the Early History of Mankind and the Development of Civilization* (Chicago: University of Chicago Press, 1864).

44. Alfred Kroeber, *Configurations of Culture Growth* (Berkeley: University of California Press, 1944).

45. Karl Bücher, *Industrial Evolution,* trans. Samuel Morley Wickett (New York: Henry Holt, 1901). For a discussion of Bücher and several other forerunners of twentieth-century communication thought, see Hanno Hardt, *Social Theories of the Press* (Boulder, Colo.: Rowman & Littlefield, 2001).

46. Innis, *Changing Concepts of Time.*

47. Anne Innis Dagg, Innis's daughter, was never privy to what this illness might have been. Anne Innis Dagg, interview by the author, Waterloo, Ontario, August 15, 2002.

Chapter Five

Time, Space, and the Oral Tradition

My bias is with the oral tradition, particularly as reflected in Greek civilization, and with the necessity of recapturing something of its spirit.

—Harold A. Innis

Innis's later work dealing with communication media is grounded in a sense of history that begins with the dawn of civilization in the ancient Near East and ends with the aftermath of World War II and the emergence of the Cold War. His approach is less concerned with chronological sequences than it is with recurring patterns and processes. The concepts he derived from studying deep history have turned out to be adaptable to the study of both the recent past and the cultural present of his own time, as well as ours. This is attested to by the influence his work is having among a growing legion of media commentators. At some point, they have all had to surmount the barrier of Innis's writing style. Some have praised it as illuminating the field in ways that might not have been possible otherwise. Students have been less impressed, often frustrated and overcome with feelings of inadequacy. Perhaps, we should confront this demon one last time before delving into the concepts that spring from it.

First, it should be stated that Innis was never a lucid writer. His early work in political economy overwhelms the reader with detail to the point where it impedes exposition, but the arguments stay their course. In the late work, it is detail that gets sacrificed to concept and the line of argumentation is rarely direct. Exasperation can easily befall the reader when, without transition, a revealing connection is broached only to be followed in the same paragraph by a leap of millennia and the introduction of a new topic.

Marshall McLuhan argues that Innis deliberately cultivated this style and that it has kinship with modernist movements such as symbolist poetry and cubist painting.[1] McLuhan also claims that his own stylistic flourishes have been so influenced and that both he and Innis write in a manner that evokes the tenets of orality. This is certainly true in McLuhan's case, since numerous passages in his writings make more sense to the ear when read aloud than they do to the eye when trying to fathom them on the page. However, the same experiment when done with Innis is likely to lead to diametric results—by all accounts his oral delivery was just as baffling to audiences as his writing. Also, the fact that Innis's writing style is nonlinear does not necessarily equate it with orality as McLuhan and others have suggested, since oral discourse can be just as linear and direct as expository writing.

Innis's writing seems rather to exist as a series of ideas lacking formal conventions we would expect to find in even the most unconventional academic prose. Not surprisingly, the notes that comprise his *Idea File* are no more confusing than several key essays in *The Bias of Communication.*[2] In a sense, a good deal of Innis's later communications writings themselves constitute an idea file—a glimpse of mind in process. We can only speculate as to why he wrote this way. Although McLuhan implies it was a deliberate strategy, this is far from certain. In the previous chapter, we did see Innis confess to being intentionally obscure when dealing with controversial subjects, but in *Bias of Communication,* the essays broaching potentially controversial issues of social critique are far more accessible than those that apply communicational concepts to history. One possible reason why his later communication studies are so note-like and sketchy is their *programmatic* nature: they outline a vast new terrain for serious scholarly research. With an urgency perhaps fueled by a sense that his health was failing, Innis must have felt that sketching the temporal and conceptual breadth of it was more important than attempting a detailed study along the lines of his earlier projects in political economy.

Be that as it may, where does this leave the student who is trying to make sense of such a gnomic and will-o'-the-wisp form of exposition? Hopefully, with a willingness to connect the dots, so to speak, over a broad range of Innis's observations. Spending a lot of time over singular passages can invite frustration. Although Innis does require interpretation, his basic ideas are accessible enough once the barrier of his style is cleared. Another potential problem in reading Innis is that he throws a wide variety of references at the reader. Since many of today's most learned academics would be unfamiliar with most of them, general readers should not feel overwhelmed. There is also no singular reading of Innis. This chapter and the next, therefore, have not been conceived as a definitive critique of his key concepts. Their purpose, rather, is to serve as a guide to the implications of some of those concepts and to encourage readers to attempt their own interpretations.

Needless to say, Innis does not provide us with ready definitions of his key terms. The very title of his most influential book, *Bias of Communication,* links the term "bias" to "communication" in an unusual way. Usually, we think of a bias the way *Merriam-Webster's Dictionary* does, as a "prejudice" or "a personal and sometimes unreasoned judgment." Innis does in fact occasionally use the term in this way, for example, when he notes that his "bias" favors Canadian nationalism or (as indicated in the epigraph to this chapter) the oral tradition. More recently, when we think of the term in relation to media, it evokes notions of biased reporting that slants news coverage toward a particular point of view, as indicated in the title of a recent book.[3]

Yet surprisingly, Innis never seems to use the term "bias" in this way. He is less concerned with issues of content—what could be described as media-bias—and more concerned with the influence the form of communication might exert over its content—what we might want to label "medium-bias." The way Innis uses the term "bias of communication" can therefore be seen as a less flamboyant precursor to McLuhan's legendary phrase "the medium is the message."

"The Bias of Communication," the title essay, tries to show rather than explain how this concept will be used to assess the relationship between media and culture, from the clay tablet to the table radio. First delivered as a 1949 lecture at the University of Michigan, the essay covers some of the same ground as "Minerva's Owl," which precedes it in the book and preceded it as a lecture by two years. Although "Bias of Communication" exhibits more thematic unity than "Minerva's Owl," each essay cites the influence of a major source as a point of departure. In "Minerva's Owl," it is Georg Hegel's use of that metaphor that sends Innis on his own historical flight. In "Bias of Communication," it is anthropologist Alfred Kroeber's ambitious but today largely forgotten *Configurations of Culture Growth* that sets Innis's historiography in motion.[4]

In addressing Kroeber's views, Innis notes that "I do not propose to do more than add a footnote to these comments and in this to discuss the significance of communication to the rise and decline of cultural traits," which he follows with perhaps the most succinct statement of his overall thesis that appears in any of his writings, "A medium of communication has an important influence in the dissemination of knowledge over space and over time and it becomes necessary to study its characteristics in order to appraise its influence in its cultural setting."[5]

He qualifies this project with another use of the term "bias," "An interest in the bias of other civilizations may itself suggest a bias of our own."[6] This intriguing observation suggests that Innis saw what he was doing in ways that we might today label "a sociology of knowledge." Further evidence for this can be found in the preface to *Bias of Communication* when he states one of his guiding precepts, which he developed from his former McMaster University professor James Ten Broeke's observation, "Why do we attend to the things to which we attend." For Innis then, learning about the past is not just an exercise in history for its own sake, it carries with it the "hope that consideration of the implications of other media to various civilizations may enable us to see more clearly the bias of our own."[7]

As a historian, Innis was very much interested in time, both as it pertains to historical movement itself and as a concept that different civilizations have exploited in a variety of ways. He even called his last book *Changing Concepts of Time*.[8] *Changing Concepts of Time* is a collection of critical essays that deals with what Innis calls "immediate problems"; but it does not discuss time in a direct way. Time is given more concerted treatment in *Bias of Communication*, especially in one of the volume's more well-known essays, "A Plea for Time," which was first presented as a lecture at the University of New Brunswick in 1950.

"Plea for Time" follows Oswald Spengler, Arnold Toynbee, and Kroeber in assuming that temporal movement in history is cyclical, "[H]istory tends to repeat itself but in the changing accents of the period in which it is written."[9] He shows little interest in notions that assume historical time is linear and illustrative of the concept of progress. A concern with time within specific historical periods is a topic he feels has been much neglected. The reason, he argues, is because most recent approaches to history are characterized on the one hand by an "obsession with the present, and on the other by the charge of antiquarianism."[10] Another way of stating this is by using the terms "presentism" and "historicism."[11] Presentism—Innis uses the term "present-mindedness"—views past events as an anticipation of, or way of informing what would come later. Historicism is history for its own sake, not quite what Innis calls "antiquarianism," but an approach that seeks to understand the significance of past events to their own time and place without regard to whether they lead to or have any bearing on what comes later. Innis rejects both extremes, or rather tries to amalgamate the strengths of each in order to achieve an approach characterized by—to use one of his favorite terms—"balance."

All past civilizations have sought in various ways to control time and space. When these two concerns are in balance, social stability results; when one or the other is overemphasized, Innis argues that collapse is inevitable, as we have seen in the previous chapter with respect to the space-biased Roman Empire.

In a given civilization, the dominant medium of communication "favors" certain forms of temporal or spatial orientation over others. For example, durable media that are difficult to transport, such as stone, clay, and parchment, impart a bias toward time rather than space. They "facilitate" an emphasis on custom, genealogical continuity, and the sacred. This impedes individualism as a dynamic for innovation, but permits it to flourish in terms of expressive communication. Time-biased civilizations also feature hierarchical social orders that allow an elite group, such as Babylonian priests or the Catholic clergy of the Middle Ages, to form a powerful class with exclusive access to a monopoly of knowledge.

At first glance, this link between the dominant medium of a civilization and its cultural orientation might seem simplistic or even idealist. A closer reading of Innis's argument, however, will reveal that when he employs the term "medium of communication," it usually does not mean only the raw material used—stone, clay, parchment, or paper—but also the *form* of communication embodied in that medium—hieroglyphics, cuneiform, or alphabetic writing. It is therefore both the medium per se, coupled with the form of communication, that predisposes the society in question to frame its knowledge of the world in particular ways. Egypt and Rome, for example, both employed papyrus, but their communications, and its consequences, were quite different because the same medium utilizing different types of script is, in effect, not the same medium. For Innis, this interest in media and communication was not the study of an autonomous aspect of culture, but an outgrowth of his earlier interest in political economy in which material factors play an important role. An obvious example of this is his concern with the economics involved in the production of a given medium and the role that medium plays in regulating the division of labor in the society employing it.

The first civilizations to be construed by Innis as time-biased were, in effect, the world's first civilizations: Sumeria, Egypt, and Babylonia. The first and third employed clay, the second (in its first incarnation), stone. He outlines the calendrical systems each developed and the role of religion in controlling the categories of time necessary to maintenance of their respective social orders. And political economist that he was, more than just the medium of communication had to be considered, "In a system of agriculture dependent on irrigation the measurement of time becomes important in predicting periods of floods and the important dates of the year, seed time and harvest."[12] In making such calculations, Babylonian civilization developed a sexigesimel system of numeration from which we derived our own use of the number sixty as a unit of clock time, along with the science of astronomy and the pseudoscience of astrology.

One of the most overt ways through which time has been subjected to social control has been through the establishment of calendars. Innis shows an abiding interest in the history of calendars, from ancient times to the modern era. Over the past generation, much interest has been shown in this topic,[13] but unfortunately the growing body of literature seems to show no awareness of Innis's earlier efforts. Exhibiting a penchant for detail that is more characteristic of his earlier work in political economy, he charts calendrical evolution from the ancient Near East, through Greece, Rome, Byzantium, the Middle Ages, and early modernity.

The Middle Ages in Europe, being under the sway of Catholicism, which used parchment as a dominant medium, were exceedingly time-biased. Calendrical time reckoning was soon expanded to include the daily measurement of time using at first the water clock and then eventually mechanical devices that brought the hour as we know it into general use and regularized the workday. This regularization of time began in the monasteries but eventually became part of the daily life of towns by the fourteenth century. One of Innis's key sources here is Lewis Mumford's *Technics and Civilization*.[14] Mumford, a nonacademic American polymath, was a twentieth century's cultural historian whose legacy and critical stance has occasionally led to comparisons with Innis.[15]

Eventually, the rise of paper and then printing brought secular interests in conflict with those of the church. Among other things, this precipitated a "struggle between church and state for control over time," which Innis explores with reference to Henry VIII and the Tudor legacy. During the French Revolution, which began in 1789, a wholesale attempt was made to do away with traditional vestiges of time by changing the names of days, months, and seasons. It resulted in an unwieldy scheme that eventually collapsed. The nineteenth century saw increasing temporal control exerted by industrialism. This gave new impetus to mechanical notions of time that led to the implementation of both standard time zones and daylight savings time by the end of the century.

The mid-twentieth century was regarded by Innis as a period of imbalance, or "present-mindedness," whereby a "[l]ack of interest in the problems of Western civilization," resulting from the space-bias of modern media, led to a situation whereby the "state has been interested in the enlargement of territories and the imposition of cultural uniformity on its peoples, and losing touch with the problems of time, has been willing to engage in wars to carry out its immediate objectives."[16] In all likelihood, he would have said the same about today's world.

For Innis, a time-bias may have characterized those hierarchical civilizations that used durable media for communications, but it was also an aspect of the oral tradition where it implied continuity with the past and a sense of tradition. A desire to recapture this spirit led him to title his essay on time in *Bias of Communication*, "A Plea for Time," while fully aware that oral societies were constrained by the "binding character of custom," which made them excessively time-bound and therefore, in Innisian terms, not completely balanced.

The examination of time and its media in the ancient, medieval, and modern worlds in *Empire and Communications,* and especially in *Bias of Communication,* is one of the most sustained topics in Innis's later work. Nevertheless, it remains at best a provocative outline that begs further elaboration, both in terms of the examples Innis cites and with respect to the possibility of including additional case studies. With respect to the latter point, it could be construed that the civilization that most epitomizes his thesis regarding time-bias is one that is never mentioned in his writings: the Maya.

Mayan history roughly spans the entirety of the first millennium A.D. Using a phonetic script with some similarities to Egyptian hieroglyphics, they wrote on the durable media of stone and parchment (if a jaguar skin can be so considered), and as Innis might have predicted they were a civilization obsessed with time. Their mathematical and astronomical skills rivaled the Babylonians and surpassed the Egyptians. Mayan scribes created a calendar of staggering complexity and accuracy—their calculation of a lunar month as 29.53020 days compares favorably to our current estimate of 29.53059 days.[17] They saw the history of the world in terms of cycles of creation and destruction—the current cycle, or long count, places the next destruction of the world on December 23, 2012.

Whether or not classic Maya civilization (A.D. 250–900) was a theocracy, thus giving it perfect conformation to the Innisian thesis, has been questioned.[18] Nevertheless, it was a hierarchical society ruled by an elite, who calculated the days and months and ordained the festival ceremonies. That Innis should have ignored a civilization so illustrative of his thesis is perhaps not surprising, given the archaeological sources he drew from—mainly British (including the British-based Australian Gordon Childe), whose perspective, largely based on Near Eastern and Asian materials, was sometimes dismissive of the significance of archaic New World civilizations to world history.

For Innis, time is an aspect of cultural orientation that the modern world needs to appreciate more fully. In "The Problem of Space," as the title of this essay in *Bias of Communication* forewarns us, space is something we have in excess that needs to be checked. As in the case of time, it has a long history that begins in the ancient world.

A concern with space arises when a civilization aspires to establish an empire. In assessing situations where the relationship between time and space shifts toward an emphasis on the latter, Innis returns again to the Near East and Egypt. A light portable medium, papyrus in this instance, is of course instrumental in facilitating such a transformation, but it was not the only factor. Before the widespread use of papyrus for administration, the geographical expanse of the Nile and the necessity of tapping it for irrigation purposes began discouraging an overly centralized administration, favoring one with more local autonomy. Papyrus greatly aided this transition, "The profound disturbances in Egyptian civilization involved in the shift from absolute monarchy to a more democratic organization coincides with a shift in emphasis on stone as a medium of communication as the basis of prestige, as shown in the pyramids, to an emphasis on papyrus."[19]

The new medium also changed the form of written communication. Elaborate hieroglyphics, with their rich visual symbolism, were suitable for stone monuments, but for the abundant new medium of papyrus their replication became laborious and inefficient. A more cursive style known as hieratic was developed. For Innis, this "marked increase in writing by hand was accompanied by a secularization of writing, thought, and activity. The social revolution between the Old and the New Kingdom was marked by a flow of eloquence and a displacement of religious by secular literature."[20] This transition seemed an intriguing anticipation of the shift from script to print that helped Europe move from the Middle Ages to modernity. He also notes how the new medium of papyrus, along with the hieratic script, helped spur the emergence of a civil service bureaucracy to help monitor the ambitions of the new kingdom. But as Egypt spread its empire, so did it become susceptible to invasion. As a result, "[c]ontrol over space was weakened, the empire contracted," because "Egyptian civilization failed to establish a stable compromise between a bias dependent on stone in the pyramids and a bias dependent on papyrus."[21]

Greece also underwent a change from a time-bias to a space-bias. The time-bias was inherent in its oral tradition. With the advent of writing, there came into being a situation of "balance" between the concerns of time and space that Innis describes in almost utopian terms. Eventually, writing got the upper hand. But before it did, there was an idyllic period when writing complemented the poetics of orality by making possible the accurate preservation of major works, such as Homer's *Iliad* and *Odyssey*. After the fifth century B.C., poetry was deemed anachronistic and prose became the narrative form of record. Along with it came written laws, with spatial thinking characterizing art, mathematics, and especially geometry. Phillip and Alexander put spatial notions into imperial practice by creating an empire that, according to Innis, eventually collapsed because of the imbalance resulting from an overemphasis on space.

Over the next several centuries, "[t]he trend of development in Rome paralleled roughly the trend described in Athens."[22] In the early days of the Roman Republic, the oral tradition, religion, and a concern with time ensured stability. As writing proliferated, along with it came the geographical conceptions of Strabo and Ptolemy, which fueled expansionist notions of the empire. This extension of statecraft used writing on papyrus—mostly obtained from Egypt—to administrate an empire that extended from Asia Minor to the Atlantic Ocean, subjecting local cultures to the dictates of imperial policy, "The Roman conquests and extension of political organization had involved the destruction of the oral tradition of the conquered and the imposition of writing."²³ This obsession with territorial acquisition, according to Innis, weakened trade and diplomacy, destabilizing the empire and allowing a new one based on parchment, religious organization, and a time-bias to rise in its stead.

During most of the Middle Ages, the Catholic Church controlled a pan-European decentralized bureaucracy and was virtually the only literate body in Europe. But eventually the Church's "monopoly over time stimulated competitive elements in the organization of space. The introduction of paper from China to Baghdad and Cordova and to Italy and France contributed to cursive writing and the organization of space in relation to the vernaculars. . . . Life could be organized legally and politically over vast territories."²⁴ With vernacular literacy and the increasing importance of trade and commerce, secular interests came to challenge those of the Church. This conflict had of course been looked at by historians previous to Innis; however, his analysis is singular in its exploration of the role of communication media, not as the cause in a deterministic sense, but as the focal point or ground on which so many elements in the debate converged.

With the advent of print, which Innis sees as the defining technology of early modernism, the spatial bias of late medievalism was accelerated. However, unlike McLuhan, whose landmark study *The Gutenberg Galaxy: The Making of Typographic Man*²⁵ argues that beginning in the fifteenth century print *brings into being* almost everything we associate with modernity—nationalism, individualism, the scientific method, and a visual orientation in our cultural logic—Innis sees print as *extending* these elements that had already been asserting themselves a century earlier. Print was also not the only medium contributing to a spatial-bias of modernity. He adds to the mix the role of the compass in the age of discovery, the telescope in opening up astronomical knowledge, and the role of mathematics and perspective in art and architecture.

In extending the notion of space-bias to the twentieth century, Innis only touches on the topic of electronic media, save for a few observations on radio and a brief mention of television, which came to Canada in December 1952, somewhat ironically one month after Innis's death. What he suggests but does not explore is that such media exacerbate the spatial-bias inherent in print by extending the influence of metropolitan centers of power. In the guise of providing greater access and democratizing knowledge, they tend to perpetuate modes of domination—especially in the case of the influence of American mass media on smaller nations, such as Canada—that in many ways resemble what took place in previous epochs. This is yet another example of cyclical inevitability of history asserting itself.

As we saw when considering Innis's views on time, his analysis of the role of media in imparting a spatial bias to various civilizations could also benefit from the inclusion of an ancient New World case study he never considered:

the Incas. At the time of Spanish contact five centuries ago, the Incas had over the previous hundred years expanded their state to create a vast empire. Based in modern-day Peru, it included parts of what are now Ecuador, Bolivia, Chile, Argentina, and Brazil. The Incas had an elaborate bureaucracy and an extensive system of communications. What they did not have was writing. Perhaps Innis, and a number of the archaeological sources he drew from, ignored the Incas because of the traditional belief that writing is a diagnostic criteria for civilization. Wrong. It is not writing per se, but some form of communication for encoding the requisite information for statecraft that can allow a society to achieve the level of complexity necessary for a civilization to form.

If we apply Innis's thesis to an expansionist empire such as the Incas, it would postulate the necessity of a light portable medium suitable for administration over distance. The Incas had just that with their quipu, a series of cords—cotton or wool—of different length, thickness, color, and patterns of braiding and knotting. Each of these elements indicated information of a certain kind. Quipus could be used to do mathematical calculations and to record such things as crop production, taxation, and a census. As Marcia Ascher and Robert Ascher argue in their impressive study *Code of the Quipu: A Study of Media Mathematics, and Culture,* the information potential of this medium compares favorably with what was possible with Sumerian clay tablet writing and the role of the quipu maker was similar to that of the scribe in the ancient Near East. Perhaps surprisingly, they cite Innis's *Empire and Communications* as a theoretical source, noting that "[h]is notion that media light in weight go with civilizations that stress space over time is supported by the Inca case."[26] The Inca civilization's fit with Innis's thesis, however, is not quite perfect, since in its space-biased quipu culture, the oral tradition, which was often linked to quipu interpretation, had the kind of importance we might expect in a more time-biased civilization.

Although time-biased civilizations normally put a greater premium on orality than those that are space-biased, their oral traditions are often constrained by a hierarchical and theocratic tradition in which elite groups control a monopoly of knowledge linked to writing. However, orality itself is for Innis a medium of communication that, if not inherently democratic, has strong leanings in that direction. It favors dialogue and resists—until the heavy hand of the state overcomes that resistance—the formation of monopolies of knowledge. Throughout his writings, he makes constant reference to the positive aspects of orality largely basing his assumptions on the Greek experience prior to the end of the fifth century B.C.

Innis was acutely aware that any understanding of orality, when archivally informed, will be imperfect, "The task of understanding a culture built on the oral tradition is impossible to students steeped in the written tradition."[27] Still, the task must be undertaken. What results could be called, following sociologist Max Weber, an "ideal type": in other words, an inductively derived model valuable as a tool in understanding the phenomenon as a general historical category, although it might not conform precisely to any specific historical example. Perhaps no one rationalized this kind of quest more eloquently than the great French philosopher Jean-Jacques Rousseau, who, in his search for the irreducible "state of nature" underscoring history, sought to "know correctly a state which no longer exists, which perhaps never existed, which probably never will exist, and about which it is nevertheless necessary to have precise notions in order to judge our present state correctly."[28]

Occasionally, Innis's ideas about orality are construed as possessing a naïveté that overstates its virtues. Eric Havelock notes that if he were to apply any "corrections of my own to Innis' work, it would be to suggest that his moral preference for the oral word is colored by a certain romanticism that history fails to justify. It is all very well to stress the oral component in Greek culture, but after all it was mainly the alphabet which released the energies of this culture into history."[29] True enough, but the oral tradition Innis actually venerates is one that owes a debt to phonetic literacy, "The alphabet escaped the implications of sacred writing. It lent itself to an efficient representation of sounds and enabled the Greeks to preserve intact a rich oral tradition."[30] It is this kind of balance between speech and writing that Innis seeks to recapture, not some lost idyllic state, when, for example, in his writings on educational reform he urges teachers to "link books to conversation and oral education" in ways that can "provide a link between a written and an oral tradition."[31]

Innis's paean to orality is heir to a legacy that dates back at least to eighteenth-century Enlightenment. Anthropologist Stanley Diamond calls this critical looking back into history for alternatives to the present the "retrospective tradition."[32] The retrospectivist does not assume historical progress is inevitable or that the period in which he or she lives is the best of all possible worlds. Part of the retrospectivist's historical mission is to find in the past not utopias, but forms of cultural expression that more fully realize our basic humanity. Rousseau was undoubtably the quintessential retrospectivist of the eighteenth century. He did not, as has been naively assumed, advocate a return to a primitive state of nature. Instead, he urged us, as Innis would urge us two centuries later, to be aware of what was lost when we contemplate both the gains of civilization and the ways we might positively reintegrate into our futures what was valuable for us in the past.

For whatever reason, Innis seems to have avoided intellectual contact with Rousseau. Possibly, he regarded the great French philosopher as a misguided romantic, or maybe he saw Rousseau's work falling within a tradition of political philosophy that had little bearing on political economy. Yet, both Innis and

Rousseau had an abiding admiration for the oral tradition. Both also wrote about education in ways that advocated a greater role for orality and a reduced emphasis on printed texts. Rousseau even went so far as to suggest that during a child's early education reading should not be taught, since he believed it impeded not only the effective oral communication, but the development of the aesthetic sensibility as well—especially regarding music (no reading here either) and art. In his "Essay on the Origins of Languages," Rousseau also comes down hard on alphabetic writing, which he calls "that dangerous supplement."[33] He argues a position more suggestive of McLuhan than Innis when he insists that inherent in the alphabet itself (rather than a result of the way this medium is used, which would be Innis's view) is a tendency to make language more analytic and less expressive, thereby leading to an emphasis on reason over the emotions.

During the nineteenth century, the retrospective tradition emerged in the writings of Karl Marx, a major social theorist who Innis confronts several times in passing but never engages directly. How aware was Innis that Marx's take on history and notions of social egalitarianism involved an appreciation of archaic societies from both classical antiquity and non-Western traditions? The following passage suggests that Innis did have a sense of Marx's leanings in that direction and that he saw his own project in ways that were not dissimilar, "My bias is with the oral tradition, particularly as reflected in Greek civilization, and with the necessity of recapturing something of its spirit. For that purpose we should try to understand something of life or of the living tradition, and the contributions of Greek civilization. Much of this will smack of the Marxian interpretation."[34]

The aspects of Marx to which Innis is referring are never made clear. Marx's major economic writings, *A Contribution to the Critique of Political Economy* and the first volume of *Capital*, both of which Innis probably read, do show an admiration for the cultural achievements of ancient Greece.[35] But Marx's ideas regarding the communist society of the future were also influenced by what the anthropological record was revealing about non-Western peoples who lived in prestate societies. As early as 1845–1846, he and Friedrich Engels, obviously influenced by Rousseau, reflected on the kind of society where an individual would not be restricted by the division of labor to a singular social role, a society where "[n]obody has one sphere of activity but each can be accomplished in any branch he wishes, society regulates the general production and thus makes it possible for me to do one thing today and Another tomorrow, to hunt in the morning, fish in the afternoon, rear cattle in the evening, criticise after dinner, just as I have a mind, without ever becoming hunter, fisherman, shepard [*sic*] or critic."[36]

Shortly before his death in 1883, Marx sought more empirical evidence for these ideas.[37] Engels followed suit with the publication of *The Origin of the Family, Private Property, and the State,* in which he synthesized a broad range of anthropological materials and compared various tribal peoples, such as the Iroquois, to the ancient Greeks.[38] However, neither Marx nor Engels discuss the oral tradition per se. What they share with Innis is a critique of the way mechanization, resulting from capitalism for Marx and Engels and misapplied technology in the case of Innis, has reduced the ability of individuals to fully participate and share in the fruits of the societies they have created, as was once possible in a number of past, but hardly utopian societies—Innis readily concedes that the Greeks he admires had slavery.

Innis's assessment of orality adds an important communication dimension to the retrospectivist tradition. But as insightful as his perspective is, it ultimately suffers from the exclusivity of constructing a model based on one source: the ancient Greeks. His work evidences no discussion of the phenomenon as evidenced in the prestate societies of sub-Saharan Africa, South Asia, and the New World. The tradition of classical scholarship he drew from, as we saw when considering time and space, favored examples that derived from Near Eastern and Greco-Roman antiquity. Unfortunately, this led him to overlook oral societies that were closer to home. Within North America, for example, Francis Parkman the historian and Lewis Henry Morgan the anthropologist discuss the oral tradition and democracy among the Iroquois.[39] Both writers favorably compare the Iroquois to the Greeks with whom Innis was so enamored. (Innis was familiar with Morgan's work on the beaver, which he cites in chapter 1 of *The Fur Trader in Canada.*[40])

At least two other important statements about orality were available at the time Innis wrote: Paul Radin's book *Primitive Man As Philosopher* and Edward Sapir's essay "Culture, Genuine, and Spurious."[41] Radin, a German American anthropologist, deals with the nature of the oral tradition and the contrast in worldview between preliterate people and those dependent on what he refers to as the "rule of the written word." Like Innis, Radin's bias is with the oral, not the written tradition; unlike Innis, Radin identifies with nonliterate tribal peoples, not the Greeks.

Sapir, an anthropological linguist, explores some of the same contrasts that would characterize Innis's later writings, such as oral versus literate and the influence of technology and mechanization on culture. Innis does quote an observation by Sapir on the complexity of primitive languages in the introduction to *Empire and Communications,* but there is no source cited for the quote or any further mention of Sapir in Innis's other writings. This is unfortunate given their geographical as well as intellectual proximity. From 1920 to 1925, Sapir was chief of the Division of Anthropology in the Geological Survey of the Canadian National Museum in Ottawa, and he published in well-known

Canadian journals, such as the *Dalhousie Review*. His fieldwork took him to western Canada at the same time Innis was pursuing his fur trade research there. In 1925, Sapir took up a post at the University of Chicago, but by that time Innis was already ensconced at the University of Toronto, where a tradition of classical scholarship, rather than anthropology, informed his concept of orality and critique of culture.

NOTES

1. McLuhan makes this argument in Marshall McLuhan, foreword to *The Bias of Communication*, by Harold A. Innis (Toronto: University of Toronto Press, 1964).

2. Harold A. Innis, *The Idea File of Harold Adams Innis,* ed. William Christian (Toronto: University of Toronto Press, 1980); Harold A. Innis, *The Bias of Communication* (1951; reprint, with an introduction by Paul Heyer and David Crowley, Toronto: University of Toronto Press, 1995).

3. Bernard Goldberg, *Bias: A CBS Insider Exposes How the Media Distorts the News* (Washington, D.C.: Regency, 2001).

4. Alfred Kroeber, *Configurations of Culture Growth* (Berkeley: University of California Press, 1944).

5. Innis, *Bias of Communication*, 33.

6. Innis, *Bias of Communication*, 33.

7. Innis, *Bias of Communication*, 34.

8. Harold A. Innis, *Changing Concepts of Time* (1952; reprint, with a foreword by James W. Carey, Boulder, Colo.: Rowman & Littlefield, 2003).

9. Innis, *Bias of Communication*, 61.

10. Innis, *Bias of Communication*, 61.

11. My use of these terms follows George W. Stocking, *Race, Culture, and Evolution: Essays in the History of Anthropology* (New York: The Free Press, 1968).

12. Innis, *Bias of Communication*, 65.

13. For example, see David Ewing Duncan, *Calendar* (New York: Avon, 1998).

14. Lewis Mumford, *Technics and Civilization* (New York: Harcourt, Brace, 1934).

15. Paul Heyer, Communications in History: Theories of Media, Knowledge, and Civilization (Westport, Conn.: Greenwood, 1988); William Kuhns, The Post-industrial Prophets: Interpretations of Technology (New York: Weybright and Talley, 1971).

16. Innis, *Bias of Communication*, 76.

17. Michael D. Coe, *The Maya* (London: Thames and Hudson, 1987), 176.

18. Coe is of the opinion that it was not.

19. Harold A. Innis, *Empire and Communications* (1950; reprint, with a foreword by Marshall McLuhan, Toronto: University of Toronto Press, 1975), 15.

20. Innis, *Empire and Communications*, 17.

21. Innis, *Bias of Communication*, 96.

22. Innis, *Bias of Communication*, 112–113.

23. Innis, *Bias of Communication*, 122.

24. Innis, *Bias of Communication*, 124.

25. Marshall McLuhan, *The Gutenberg Galaxy: The Making of a Typographic Man* (New York: Signet, 1969).

26. Marcia Ascher and Robert Ascher, *Code of the Quipu: A Study in Media, Mathematics, and Culture* (Ann Arbor: University of Michigan Press, 1981), 59.

27. Innis, Empire and Communications, 55.

28. Jean-Jacques Rousseau, "The Discourse on the Origin and Foundation of Inequality among Men," in *Jean-Jacques Rousseau: The First and Second Discourses*, ed. Roger D. Masters (New York: St. Martin's, 1964), 93.

29. Eric Havelock, *Harold A. Innis: A Memoir* (Toronto: The Harold Innis Foundation, 1982), 42.

30. Innis, *Empire and Communications*, 53.

31. Innis, *Bias of Communication*, 214.

32. Stanley Diamond, *The Search for the Primitive: A Critique of Civilization* (New Brunswick, N.J.: Transaction, 1974).

33. Jean-Jacques Rousseau and Johann Gottfried Herder, *On the Origin of Language* (New York: Unger, 1966), 19.

34. Innis, *Bias of Communication*, 190.

35. Karl Marx, *A Contribution to the Critique of Political Economy*, trans. Nahum I. Stone (1859; reprint New York: International, 1970); Karl Marx, *Capital*, vol. 1 (1867; reprint New York: International, 1972).

36. Karl Marx and Friedrich Engels, *The German Ideology* (New York: International, 1972), 53.

37. For example, see Karl Marx, *The Ethnological Notebooks of Karl Marx*, ed. and trans. Lawrence Krader (Assen, The Netherlands: Van Gorcum, 1972).

38. Friedrich Engels, *The Origin of the Family, Private Property, and the State* (1884; reprint, Chicago: Kerr, 1902).

39. For example, see Francis Parkman, *Francis Parkman's Works* (Toronto: Morceny, 1900); Lewis Henry Morgan, *League of the Ho-de-no-sau-nee or Iroquois* (New York: Franklin, 1862).

40. Harold A. Innis, *The Fur Trade in Canada* (1930; reprint, New Haven, Conn.: Yale University Press, 1962).

41. Paul Radin, *Primitive Man As Philosopher* (New York: Appleton, 1927); Edward Sapir, "Culture, Genuine, and Spurious," *American Journal of Sociology* 29 (1924).

Chapter Six

Monopolies of Knowledge and the Critique of Culture

> Mechanization has emphasized complexity and confusion; it has been responsible for monopolies in the field of knowledge.
>
> —Harold A. Innis

Innis saw his work in media history as providing the foundation for a critical assessment of a world ravaged by two global conflicts and now beset on by the mechanizing tendencies of mass media and unchecked commercialism. The seeds of what could be called his critical social theory were, of course, sown earlier. Political economy had shown him that the past was rife with inequities based on opportunism and greed. But Canadian economic history was too limited a basis on which to build an indictment of the present. A half century earlier, when Thorstein Veblen, one of his major influences, was called to the task, he drew liberally from world history and anthropology. Innis now had a substantial arsenal of information from at least the former area. Using the past to measure the present, however, is a task that needs careful qualification, "We must all be aware of the extraordinary, perhaps insuperable difficulty in assessing the quality of a culture of which we are a part of or of assessing the quality of a culture of which we are not a part. In using other cultures as mirrors in which we may see our own culture we are affected by the astigmatism of our own eyesight and the defects of the mirror, with the result that we are apt to see nothing in other cultures but the virtues of our own."[1]

Although modernity has unleashed on the world great benefits, Innis suggests that it has also not delivered on all its promises, "The conditions of freedom of thought are in danger of being destroyed by science, technology, and the mechanization of knowledge, and with them Western civilization."[2] He questions the arrogance that assumes we are somehow outside history or have finally transcended it. As was the case with Egypt, Babylonia, and Rome, we, too, might be headed for a fall, since the biases that made those ancient civilizations vulnerable to collapse are not altogether absent from our own. There are, for example, monopolies of knowledge in our culture that make it less "flexible" than we assume it to be. His assessment of how such constraints operated in past civilizations, therefore, is not intended to arrogantly show, as Georg Hegel tried to, the degree to which we have shed them, but quite the opposite.

"Monopoly of knowledge" thus becomes a crucial term in Innis's later writings. Not surprisingly, he provides no formal definition save to suggest that it is an extension of "concepts in the special field of economics, and in particular the concept of monopoly," to the field of knowledge.[3] The term is used broadly, to cover what we would normally classify as knowledge per se, literacy and science, for example, and what is more generally assumed to be information, such as economic records and census data. Sometimes, more specific economic factors, such as transportation and the organization of markets, are subsumed under the monopoly of knowledge rubric.

It seems to be a given for Innis that monopolies of knowledge are nearly impossible in cultures where the dominant mode of communication is the spoken word. Although this might be true to a degree, something akin to a monopoly of knowledge is possible in an oral culture: for example, when a given individual, such as a skilled hunter or shaman, knows something the average person does not and controls access to it in an authoritative way. Such scenarios, although possible, are exceedingly rare.[4] However, it would be accurate to say that in oral cultures, class-based monopolies of knowledge are virtually impossible—situations, in other words, where major segments of the society, such as scribe priests, control a substantial body of lore essential to the overall operation the society. Innis would probably not put it this way, since given his uneasy relationship with Karl Marx he avoids completely using social class as an analytical concept. What he does emphasize in the introduction to *Empire and Communications* is the role of writing as a prerequisite for the formation of a monopoly of knowledge. It

> provided a justification for established authority. An extended social structure strengthened the position of an individual leader with military power who gave orders to agents who received and executed them. The sword and pen worked together. Power was increased by concentration in a few hands, specialization of function was enforced, and scribes with leisure to keep and Records contributed to the advancement of knowledge and thought. The written record signed, sealed, and swiftly transmitted was essential to military power and the extensions of government. Small communities were written into states and states were consolidated into empire.[5]

In Egypt, when writing first began on stone, the Pharaohs and their scribe priests possessed a powerful monopoly of knowledge to which the masses were obligated. After 2000 B.C., with the arrival of papyrus, the "Pharaohs gave up their monopoly and accepted the extension of rights to the whole population."[6] The subsequent expansion of Egyptian civilization led to warfare through which Egyptian "hegemony" (a term usually associated with the critical social theory of Antonio Gramsci, a Marxist whom Innis does not cite) made use of a monopoly of knowledge over the people they had subjugated and over their own people in terms of the military conscription necessary to expand their empire. In Babylonia, a complex apprenticeship was also associated with writing, bringing it under the stewardship of a favored class. Innis's assessment of how Babylonian scribe priests used their monopoly of knowledge to effect the mathematical, legal, and military control essential to the establishment of empire is much indebted to Gordon Childe, as we saw in the previous chapter.

In Greece, the relative ease in learning the alphabet, compared to the protracted apprenticeship necessary for literacy in Egypt and Babylonia, did not at first favor monopolistic control. The initial situation of balance between Greek oral and literate traditions, however, eventually ended with the rise of complex written laws leading to "oppressive features in judicial control and the levying of tribute."[7] Rome followed suit, and although literacy was widespread there, the empire used the vast collection of written works it had acquired more for display status than for learning; writing itself became increasingly directed toward the codification of more complex laws. The subsequent Middle Ages, with its "monopoly of knowledge built up under ecclesiastical control," was even more restrictive.[8] Here, the scribe priests controlled not only the acquisition of literacy and production of parchment, but also the copying of texts deemed to be "knowledge" and the suppression or destruction of those held to be otherwise. A vivid dramatization of this can be found in both the novel and film versions of Umberto Eco's *The Name of the Rose*.[9]

Paper eventually challenged the parchment-dependent monopoly of knowledge of the Catholic Church, and by the sixteenth century print had made scribes, both monastic and secular, virtually obsolete. But in Innis's view, since monopolies of knowledge appear to be inevitable to the process of historical formation, what typography giveth, it would also taketh away. Censorship laws and the economic monopolies enjoyed by various publishers became a problem, a result of the "enormous expansion of the printing industry and an emphasis on freedom of the press, which favoured the growth of monopolies."[10]

Innis deals only briefly with the twentieth century. In the revealing essay "Technology and Public Opinion in the United States," he looks at the "monopoly position of the Associated Press" and its subsequent collision with William Randolph Hearst, along with Hearst's own newspaper chain-building aspirations.[11] Innis also senses a shift in the mass media that has generated much comment in recent years. Where once media monopolies could be directly linked to political interests, now there was another agenda, one he saw powerfully influencing Canada. In the first essay in *Changing Concepts of Time*, "The Strategy of Culture," he notes that "[w]e are fighting for our lives. The pernicious influence of American advertising reflected especially in the periodical press and the powerful persistent impact of commercialism have been evident in all the ramifications of Canadian life."[12] He also observes how much of Canadian publishing at the time was controlled by American and British parent companies, with Canadian writers and publishers forced to emulate their standards in order to compete. This is not exactly a "monopoly of knowledge" per se, although he still uses this term in an all inclusive way, but something more along the lines of information control on behalf of American, and to a lesser extent British, commercial capitalism.[13]

"The Strategy of Culture" further explores these ideas. Although Innis is primarily concerned with the erosion of Canadian culture through the force of American publishing, he does note that American culture itself has become victim to its own commercial excesses. He points out how publishing in his adopted city of Chicago has been marginalized and disadvantaged by a commercial centralism favoring New York. Innis also lauds the challenge to crass commercial publishing posed by "quality magazines," such as H. L. Mencken's *American Mercury,* but Mencken's periodical was far more commercially viable in a wealthy nation such as the United States than similar experiments could be in Canada. Government assistance, Innis believes, is sorely needed to bolster the Canadian cultural industries. He thus regards the establishment of the Canadian Broadcasting Corporation and National Film Board as positive steps; however, his hope that these institutions would play a more prominent role in Canadian culture during the upcoming television age has not been fulfilled.

For Innis, the techniques of advertising and mass persuasion, which he argues were refined during the propaganda campaigns of World War I, pose a potent danger to both Canadian and American culture. Canada, in return for providing the United States with abundant and inexpensive pulp and paper, in turn imports inexpensive magazines and potboilers that express an American point of view as much through their advertising as through the texts it supports. One wonders—but not for long—what Innis might say in response to the debate currently raging in Canada that has resulted from the North American Free Trade Agreement being applied to periodical publishing. Many split-run magazines are sold in Canada, which are token Canadian editions of their U.S. counterparts and feature Canadian advertising. Supported by an enormous income from their American sales and advertising revenue, they are able to charge low rates for Canadian advertisers. This drains valuable advertising support from an already precarious Canadian publishing industry. Writing more than a half century ago, Innis insisted that Canadian's "can only survive by taking persistent action against American imperialism in all its attractive guises," and that such action might in turn benefit those against whom it is directed "[b]y attempting constructive efforts to explore the cultural possibilities of various media of communication and to develop them along lines free from commercialism, Canadians might make a contribution to the cultural life of the United States by releasing it from dependence on the sale of tobacco and other commodities."[14]

Part of the danger Innis associates with the spread of American cultural influence is the United States' rootedness in militarism. In *Changing Concepts of Time,* he discusses this in the essay "Military Implications of the American Constitution," which is unsettling and prescient in light of today's geopolitics. Playing the role of an outsider peering in at American culture, a role he likens to Alexis de Tocqueville, the Frenchman, and Lord Bryce, the Englishman, Innis traces the history of American militarism by looking at the policies of the presidency from George Washington to the eve of Dwight D. Eisenhower.

Innis echoes long-standing Canadian concerns regarding American expansionism. Born of the unsuccessful American invasion of Canada during the War of 1812, and exacerbated by the Monroe Doctrine (1823), which justified the annexation of Texas and California, American "manifest destiny" eyed Canada throughout much of the nineteenth century. In assessing the Spanish-American War (1898), Innis cites Henry Cabot Lodge's exhortation at the time that "[f]rom the Rio Grande to the Arctic Ocean there should be but one flag and one country."[15] During the twentieth century, he concedes that American designs on Canada have been more cultural than political. However, with the Cold War in full swing at the time he wrote, he urged Canada to find the courage to stay its own course and not reflexively follow American policy dictates, "We have never had the courage of Yugoslavia in relation to Russia and we have never produced a Tito."[16] The issue of Canada's position with respect to the United States' foreign policy has never been as scrutinized as it has been of late with respect to the Middle East.

The foregoing critique Innis developed with respect to the culture of his own time and place was not the result of a sudden aversion, but was arrived at after much historical reflection. In *Bias of Communication,* he writes that "[i]t is perhaps a unique characteristic of civilization that each civilization believes in its own uniqueness and superiority to other civilizations. Indeed this may be the meaning of culture—i.e., some which we have that others have not."[17] Possibly, he derived this notion from a Greek writer he might have read or read about. In his *Histories,* Herodotus, when commenting on the lifeways of non-Greek peoples, often begins his sentences with "They do not have,"

"Contrary to us they do not," and so on. What Innis is implying or warning against here is the danger of ethnocentrism (a word he does not use), the notion that one's own culture is the measure by which all others must be judged.

There are, of course, many ways to define culture. Given his interest in classical scholarship, Innis seems to subscribe to the humanist view, which sees culture as those transcendent outpourings of society that include art, architecture, religion, and philosophy. A social science perspective would regard culture more as everyday lived experience—such as values, habits, customs, folkways, and much of what we now refer to as popular culture, in order to distinguish it from "high" or humanist culture.

Innis notes how a culture's architecture and sculpture can exude prestige and be an index of power, for example, as in the case of the Egyptian pyramids. Imperial power was also demonstrated in the great libraries of antiquity, such as Alexandria, Rome, and more recently, as he points out, Washington, D.C. These extremes prompt the question regarding what form of culture might constitute an ideal, which often arises when a humanist position on the culture concept is considered. Innis naturally sides with the Greeks, whose culture "escaped the centralizing tendencies of river civilizations with their effects on capitals, architecture, and writing with its implications for bureaucracy."[18]

This was a culture with a maxim of "nothing in excess," which, when it eventually succumbed to the "growth of writing and individualism," aspired to be an empire, attained that status, and then eventually collapsed.

With the advent of print in the fifteenth century, momentous changes occurred in the history of Western culture. Science and technology flourished, and along with it a visual emphasis. Innis (not without a bit of sarcasm) sees print as responsible for the claim that what "has been ushered in" is "a new and superior civilization. No civilization, we are told, has enjoyed our advantages. Democracy, education, progress, individualism, and other blessed words describe our new heaven."[19] He urges us not to be overawed by this new technology, lest we lose our objectivity, for in its wake print has also bequeath to us machine industry and specialism, which in the guise of liberating Western civilization has created new monopolies and social constraints.

One of the major consequences of print, machine industry, and specialism is mechanization. Innis regards it as a process operating and originating in technology, a process that has now permeated almost every facet of our social arrangements and cultural values. His work here shows strong kinship with a tradition of technological criticism that includes writers such as Sigfried Giedion (whose 1948 book *Mechanization Takes Command: A Contribution to Anonymous History* is not cited), Jacques Ellul (who wrote after Innis), and Lewis Mumford (whose 1934 classic *Technics and Civilization* is cited in the early but not the later Innis).[20] When discussing the impact of mechanization of culture, his most immediate influence, a source cited with much approval, is Graham Wallas's *Social Judgment*.[21]

Following Wallas, Innis attributes to mechanization a de-emphasis on oral communication, "Reading is quicker than listening and concentrated individual thought than verbal exposition and counter exposition of arguments. The printing press and the radio address the world instead of the individual."[22] Innis also cites Arthur Schopenauer's warning regarding books as an impediment to thought. He might also have mentioned Søren Kierkegaard and Friedrich Nietzsche, who espoused a similar view—in their books of course. It may seem ironic that an academic as dependent on the printed word as Innis would chastise the hand on which so much of his handiwork depended. His views do seem extreme, but he is no Luddite with respect to either books or machines. His goal is balance. Although he offers only a few ambiguous answers, the abiding question is clear enough: Since the gains wrought by communication technology and mechanization have been accompanied by losses, how can we minimize the latter and still make full human use of the former?

In the context of his historiography, this may seem like armchair theorizing. In the context of his lived experience as an academic leader, it was not. Innis's critique of culture addressed education directly. The university itself he saw as a kind of corporation, often hoarding its own monopoly of knowledge. To make this knowledge more accessible, he took a proactive position well before he began to write formally about communication and culture. From the outset of his academic career, he was involved in programs of adult continuing education—many of his students in the early 1920s were war veterans who he felt should not be denied the educational resources of the university. Toward the end of his life, he became involved with a royal commission that studied adult education, although his observations were far from consonant with those of the bureaucrats to whom he was accountable.

Postsecondary education is deemed by Innis to be unduly conservative. He reminds us that the "whole external history of science is a history of the resistence [*sic*] of academies and universities to the progress of knowledge."[23] There was, as he sees it, too much emphasis on rote learning and not enough on critical thinking. He advocates that universities "subject their views about their role in civilization to a systematic overhauling" and that those who teach "should be encouraged to write books as a means of compelling them to give new lectures."[24] The latter point may seem ironic, if not downright contradictory, given his critique of the book and advocacy of a greater role in education for oral discourse. However, it does make overall sense given that his ultimate goal is pedagogical balance. He seems to be saying that academics should write books, not in response to a publish or perish mandate, or to produce authorita-

tive texts for posterity, but to make them better and more informed teachers—
the written word serving the spoken, as was the case in the period of Greek
civilization he so admired.

In his critique of education, another Hellenistic ideal looms prominent, "We
should, then, be concerned like the Greeks with making men, not overwhelming them by facts."[25] He therefore advocates a broad-based curriculum that
avoids excessive specialization (no mention, however, of gymnastics and music,
essential components of Greek pedagogy). Education should not be afraid to
confront major philosophical problems in Western civilization and especially
abstract ideas, which he sees as often "ground down to convenient size" by
"print, radio, and film," so as to "meet the demands of large numbers."[26]

Sharp criticism is leveled at the examination system, which is seen as a prime
example of "mechanism" in education. It tends to favor students from large
urban areas and middle-class backgrounds, disadvantaging students from districts that cannot attract the best teachers and latest equipment. He cites the
higher failure rate of students from rural schools as a consequence. Clearly,
Innis is invoking his own early experiences, perhaps recalling the difficulties he
was ill prepared to surmount when he first arrived at Woodstock Collegiate.
The divide he sees between urban and rural education is not without contemporary resonance if we transpose it to the gap that often exists between affluent
suburban and less well endowed inner-city school districts.

There is also in Innis's writings on education an elitism that has puzzled
some commentators. He states that "[u]niversities must strive to enlist the most
active energetic minds to train the most active energetic minds."[27] Only the
"ablest students" should be admitted to university, although the criteria on
which to make such admissions is not spelled out. It would seem, although he
is never quite clear on this, that the university should be open to all—cost or a
socially disadvantaged background should not be a limiting factor. However,
given the standards he feels the university should uphold and the challenges it
should pose to students—in creative thinking not rote learning—only those
with the requisite talent and level of commitment need apply. For individuals
lacking this wherewithal, there are worthy alternatives. He does not spell out
what they are, but he does feel strongly that programs of adult education
should be nurtured in order to make the resources of the university widely
accessible to those not pursuing a formal degree-based program.

The curriculum itself—he advocates primarily on behalf of arts programs—
should have both critical scholarly quality and social relevance, "Students and
Staff should concentrate on the development of capacities to resist the influence of mechanization and to make free contributions to the solution of the
age-old problems of Western civilization."[28] Long-held assumptions must be
questioned. A "philosophical approach" should be cultivated that resists dogma

and extremism. Such a vision, he well realized, would in all likelihood be hamstrung by bureaucrats. He therefore argues on behalf of a European model whereby the university would be self-governed by scholars with administrators and the wider community maintaining an arms-length relationship. Administrators can, however, take an active role in overseeing programs of adult education, *provided* that such programs do not become mere cash cows whose purpose is to offer up a formulaic curriculum in order to promote goodwill, which he sees as the university succumbing to the tenets of the marketplace. These programs should draw from the best resources of the university and be a means of opening dialogue with the public. They should emphasize the importance of an "oral education," to be served by, not subservient to, printed texts. Noble ideals to be sure, but he had been leading by example for almost thirty years.

NOTES

1. Harold A. Innis, *The Bias of Communication* (1951; reprint, with an introduction by Paul Heyer and David Crowley, Toronto: University of Toronto Press, 1995), 132.

2. Innis, *Bias of Communication,* 190.

3. Harold A. Innis, "The Concept of Monopoly and Civilization" (1951), in *Staples, Markets, and Cultural Change: Harold Innis,* ed. Daniel Drache (Montreal: McGill-Queens University Press, 1995).

4. For a thorough discussion of the dynamics of such societies, see Stanley Diamond, *The Search for the Primitive* (New Brunswick, N.J.: Transaction, 1974).

5. Harold A. Innis, *Empire and Communications* (1950; reprint, with a foreword by Marshall McLuhan, Toronto: University of Toronto Press, 1975), 10.

6. Innis, *Empire and Communications,* 15.

7. Innis, *Empire and Communications,* 82.

8. Innis, *Empire and Communications,* 139.

9. Umberto Eco, *The Name of the Rose,* trans. William Weaver (San Diego: Harcourt Brace Jovanovich, 1983); Umberto Eco, *The Name of the Rose,* dir. Jean-Jacques Annaud (20th Century Fox Film Corporation, 1986).

10. Innis, *Empire and Communications,* 167.

11. Innis, *Bias of Communication.*

12. Harold A. Innis, *Changing Concepts of Time* (Toronto: University of Toronto Press, 1952), 19; see also the new edition, Harold A. Innis, *Changing Concepts of Time* (with a foreword by James W. Carey, Boulder, Colo.: Rowman & Littlefield, 2003).

13. Although he uses the term "capitalism" in his early economic writings, he does not employ it in the critique of culture found in the later communication studies.

14. Innis, *Changing Concepts of Time,* 20.

15. Innis, *Changing Concepts of Time,* 33.

16. Innis, *Changing Concepts of Time,* 45.

17. Innis, *Bias of Communication,* 132.

18. Innis, *Bias of Communication,* 136.

19. Innis, *Bias of Communication,* 139.

20. Sigfried Giedion, *Mechanization Takes Command: A Contribution to Anonymous History* (New York: Oxford University Press, 1948); Jacques Ellul, *The Technological Society* (New York: Knopf, 1964); Lewis Mumford, *Technics and Civilization* (New York: Harcourt Brace, 1934). For comparisons between their work and Innis's, see William Kuhns, *The Post-Industrial Prophets: Interpretations of Technology* (New York: Weybright and Talley, 1971).

21. Graham Wallas, *Social Judgment* (London: Allen and Unwin, 1934).

22. Innis, *Bias of Communication,* 191.

23. Innis, *Bias of Communication,* 194.

24. Innis, *Bias of Communication,* 195.

25. Innis, *Bias of Communication,* 203.

26. Innis, *Bias of Communication,* 204–205.

27. Innis, *Bias of Communication,* 209.

28. Innis, *Bias of Communication,* 209.

Chapter Seven

An Enduring Legacy

I think there are lines appearing in *Empire and Communications,* for example,
which suggest the possibility of organizing an entire school of studies.

—Marshall McLuhan to Harold A. Innis, March 14, 1951

Following Innis's death in 1952, most eulogies honored him for his work in
political economy. Even in Canada, numerous colleagues were perplexed by
his later communication studies. Some saw it as an indulgent preoccupation of
his later years—a foray into a nonexistent (in Canada) field that seemed to pose
a cloudy barrier to his true, staples theory persona. But there were notable
exceptions and communication studies at the University of Toronto did not
die with Innis.

Before he became the charismatic "oracle of the electronic media" during
the 1960s, Marshall McLuhan had been approaching the subject of communications from the direction of literary criticism. Innis knew little if anything
about literary modernists such as Stéphane Mallarmé, William Butler Yeats,
James Joyce, Ezra Pound, and T. S. Eliot, who so inspired McLuhan and whose
influence underscored his first book, *The Mechanical Bride: Folklore of Industrial
Man.* In this study, the poetic hype of advertising is turned back on itself in a
telling critique. We also find a McLuhan quite different from the "medium is
the message" prophet who emerged a decade later.[1]

There is no question that Innis thought highly of *Mechanical Bride.* He even
gave a copy of it to his son Hugh as a Christmas present, a gift the young man
found quite perplexing.[2] *Mechanical Bride* and Innis's *The Bias of Communication*
not only came out the same year, they evidence a remarkably similar critical
sensibility.[3] McLuhan's full-blown critique of commercial culture, circa 1950,
seems to amplify the handful of observations on this topic that we find in *Bias
of Communication,* especially in essays such as "Industrialism and Cultural Values" and "A Critical Review." McLuhan's project, however, had been in the

85

works several years before he was aware of his colleague's penchant for media studies. It seems probable that the happy coincidence of their books appearing the same year possibly helped spur McLuhan on in this direction.

Just prior to the publication of *Bias of Communication,* McLuhan indicated an awareness and appreciation of Innis's work in a letter to his colleague from which the epigraph to this chapter was taken. In this lengthy epistle (four single-spaced pages), McLuhan discusses his literary sources and their relevance to Innis's research. Innis thanked McLuhan and indicated that he would like to circulate the letter among "one or two mutual friends."[4] In all probability, Innis was unfamiliar, except by name, with the writers cited by McLuhan. McLuhan must have sensed this, though the tone of his correspondence assumes a basic awareness of the major works of the literary figures previously mentioned. Later, in a letter to William Kuhns dated December 6, 1971, he notes that Innis "had no training in the arts, and this was his gross defect."[5]

This defect notwithstanding, McLuhan became an insistent if not always consistent promoter of Innis. More than a few researchers "discovered" Innis because of McLuhan's exhortations regarding the importance of his former colleague's work. In his 1962 book *The Gutenberg Galaxy: The Making of a Typographic Man,* McLuhan cites Innis's observations on the importance of both the phonetic alphabet on antiquity and print on modernity. He declares that "Innis was the first person to hit upon the *process* of change as implicit in the *forms* of media technology. The present book is a footnote of explanation to his work."[6] It is more than that. *Gutenberg Galaxy* is a comprehensive, if somewhat controversial, recasting of the vision of communications history outlined in *Empire and Communications.* However, by this point McLuhan had already jettisoned the critical stance he had shared with Innis a decade earlier.

. Innis is also championed in the forewords McLuhan wrote during the 1970s to paperback editions of *Empire and Communications* and *Bias of Communication.* In *Empire and Communications,* he reiterates what he said in *Gutenberg Galaxy,* "I am pleased to think of my own book, *The Gutenberg Galaxy,* as a footnote to the observations of Innis on the subject of the psychic and social consequences, first of writing and then of printing," and goes on to praise a book in which "[e]ach sentence is a compressed monograph."[7]

His foreword to *Bias of Communication* begins in a similar laudatory fashion, but quickly lapses into several misunderstandings. The most notable one perhaps being the contention—which serves to diminish Innis's originality—that Innis was strongly influenced by sociologist Robert Ezra Park and can be seen as a member of the Chicago School in which Park was a leading figure. As we saw in chapter 1, American communications scholar James W. Carey questions this notion.

Although they were kindred spirits of a sort in their intellectual vision

quests, the personalities of Innis and McLuhan could not have been more diametric. Innis, still the Baptist, if not in religious belief, certainly in his self-
discipline and an austere lifestyle that included the most basic home furnish-
ings, but also a bit of radio on Sunday night, Jack Benny and Fred Allen, and
on rare occasions a movie outing—his daughter Anne Innis Dagg recalls his
fondness for the Marx brothers.[8] Although his work was critical and at times
moralistic, it was not without a wry sense of both humor and irony, elements
McLuhan appreciated, although his own effort in those directions depended
more on poetical word play, whereas Innis tended to cite historical situations.

They met but a few times. Hearsay in Canadian academe suggests that those
meetings were brief, formal, and at times almost strained. McLuhan, the flamboyant born-again Catholic, was open to the various forms of popular culture
(even though he had been critical of them in *Mechanical Bride*) that Innis found
anathema. Anthropologist Edmund Carpenter, a colleague of McLuhan's at the
University of Toronto during the 1950s, observed both men firsthand:

> Differences between McLuhan & Innis were unbridgeable, though their writings cov-
> ered much the same ground and employed much the same style. . . . Marshall talked
> on and on, at one point drifting into politics. Innis detested dictators, monopolies,
> censorship, racism. He was firmly committed to an open society. Marshall was just as
> firmly committed to a closed society. . . . Marshall loved America's "cornucopia of
> surrealism." He thought Canadians were missing out on a good thing. Innis feared its
> impact on Canadian identity. . . . The gap between them was wide, the difference say
> between Frost & Pound. Harold Innis was a social model. He personified reason, jus-
> tice, democracy. When he spoke he seemed to speak for society. Marshall spoke for
> himself.[9]

Carpenter appreciated the work of both men. In 1953, he conceived, edited,
and marketed *Explorations,* an exciting and unconventional interdisciplinary
journal devoted to the study of human communication. It ran more or less
annually until 1959. The list of contributors from a variety of disciplines is
impressive and the journal has achieved near legendary status among students
of communication. McLuhan eventually came on board as a coeditor a year
later. The 1954 issue (*Explorations Three*) features a previously unpublished lecture by Innis, "The Concept of Monopoly and Civilization," with an introduction by Innis's colleague W. T. Easterbrook. The source for the lecture is
not indicated, but it was originally delivered in Paris on July 6, 1951, at a symposium chaired by the historian Lucien Febvre. In the brief introduction, Easterbrook strongly hints that Innis's "History of Communications" manuscript
will eventually be published, an event we are still waiting for a half-century
later.

Explorations went in artistic directions that might have puzzled Innis and his name is usually not mentioned when discussions of the it are broached. Nevertheless, his influence on *Explorations* can be seen in this later reflection by Carpenter on the mandate of the journal, "*Explorations* focused on media biases. This concern rested on the belief that certain media favor, while others do not, certain ideas and values, or more simply: each medium is a unique soil. That soil doesn't guarantee which plants will grow there, but it influences which plants blossom or wilt there."[10]

By the 1960s, sometimes owing to McLuhan's citations, sometimes not, Innis's name began appearing in various media-related discussions. One of the most surprising commentaries on his work appears in John Houseman's opening address as Regent's Lecturer in the Department of Theater and Film at the University of California, Los Angeles (UCLA), in 1963.[11] Houseman is usually remembered today for his Best Supporting Actor Oscar for *The Paper Chase* (1973), his acting debut at age seventy, and for a series of television commercials he did in the 1970s and 1980s. However, prior to assuming the post at UCLA he had a long career in a variety of the performing arts. Of note is his work with Orson Welles' Mercury Theatre on stage and in radio (Houseman coproduced the infamous *War of the Worlds* "panic broadcast" in 1938); he was also the producer of such acclaimed Hollywood films as *The Blue Dahlia* (1946), *The Bad and the Beautiful* (1952), and *Julius Caesar* (1953); and for two years he produced one of the most highly acclaimed programs in the history of television: *Playhouse 90*.

In the Regent's Lecture, Houseman discusses the relationship among the performing arts, entertainment, and the mass media. In doing so, he invokes the work of a "Canadian scholar, a man of wonderful ideas but forbidding style, Harold A. Innis."[12] Using *Bias of Communication* as his source, Houseman gives a brief overview of Innis's approach to media history emphasizing the Canadian's take on the role of mechanization in the formation of "monopolies in communication." Not surprisingly, given his theater background, Houseman appreciates Innis's assessment of the spoken word, "It was one of Innis's theories that civilizations where oral and vernacular communication prevail, such as classical Athens, or the England of Elizabeth, tend to be superior in spiritual and political vitality to those in which a rigid written or codified tradition of learning have facilitated monopolistic control and a deliberate freezing of the means of communication."[13]

Houseman goes on to use Innis to develop a critique of "commercial opportunism" masquerading as democracy in popular entertainment. Adapting Innis's notion of balance, he makes a plea for the incorporation of more high-quality fare into television, a medium he sees as receding rapidly from the Golden Age of programming that characterized the previous decade—especially when *Playhouse 90* was canceled and replaced with *The Beverly Hillbillies*.

Following the interest in media studies generated during the 1960s by the success of McLuhan's *Understanding Media: The Extensions of Man*, references to Innis began to appear more frequently. McLuhan critiques also became a cottage industry both within and outside academe. One such critique also embraced Innis, and in doing so has become a definitive introduction to his work. In 1967, James Carey, then at the University of Illinois, published an essay in the *Antioch Review* titled "Harold Adams Innis and Marshall McLuhan."[14]

In 1967, an article about Innis sans the comparison with McLuhan would have generated little interest, as Carey must have known. His respectful but stern critique of McLuhan is accompanied by an assessment of Innis that argues not only for Innis's priority in recognizing the centrality on communication technology, but also that he did a better job at comprehending it. In a later essay, Carey playfully challenges the notion that a major vector in communication thought runs from Innis to McLuhan by quoting Oscar Wilde's response when viewing the Niagara Falls for the first time, "It would be more impressive," he is reputed to have said, "if it ran the other way."[15] The 1967 essay, while conceding important similarities between the two Canadian communication theorists, clearly defines an important difference in their respective agendas, "Whereas Innis sees communication technology principally affecting social organization and culture, McLuhan sees its principal effect on sensory organization and thought. McLuhan has much to say about perception and thought but little to say about institutions. Innis has much to say about institutions and little to say about perception and thought."[16]

Carey appraises Innis's early work in political economy and sees the later communication studies as emerging from these concerns. He notes how Innis's style, which he calls a "psychedelic delicatessen," poses a barrier to readers but also allows them to make connections that would have perhaps been impossible if a more conventional format had been followed. Carey does not shrink from calling Innis a technological determinist, but in comparing him to McLuhan, Innis is regarded as a "soft determinist." Innis's historiography is assessed in sympathetic terms, as are his ideas regarding time and space, the oral tradition, and monopolies of knowledge. Links are made to the concept of authority in the works of sociologist Max Weber, with whom it now seems Innis was unfamiliar.

In each subsequent decade, Carey published essays that discuss Innis's relationship to the Chicago School, American geographic thought, and more recent trends in communication studies. Most Innis commentators of the past and current generation regard Carey's work as both a benchmark in Innis scholarship and a starting point for further assessments of his legacy. Carey's appreciation of Innis, however, is not limited to commentary. As indicated by the title of his 1989 essay collection *Communication As Culture: Essays on Media and Society,* he incorporates Innisian notions into an original perspective on media and modernity.[17] Of note is his essay "Technology and Ideology: The Case of the Telegraph," which provides a revealing assessment of an important communication technology Innis only mentions in passing. Most recently, Carey contributed a foreword to the 2003 edition of Innis's last book, *Changing Concepts of Time.*

In 1968, Jack Goody published the important anthology *Literacy in Traditional Societies.*[18] "The Consequences of Literacy" (first published in 1963), the introductory essay, has been much cited and responsible for stimulating anthropological interest in this topic. Goody subsequently wrote two related books, *The Domestication of the Savage Mind* and *The Logic of Writing and the Organization of Society.*[19] In their original essay, Goody and Ian Watt cite Innis's *Bias of Communication* in an expanded footnote that also discusses *Empire and Communications* and the journal *Explorations* as important contributions to the cross-cultural and historical study of communication.

Goody and Watt's essay may have also been the first reference to Innis, McLuhan (to whom they are less favorably disposed), and Eric Havelock as part of a "Toronto School" of communication studies.[20] The term has endured, but not without controversy. What constitutes a "school" in the tradition of academe and whose prerogative is it to define one? Can what happened intellectually in Toronto be compared to the Chicago School in this regard? Should Innis, a critical social theorist, be even seen as sharing a tradition with McLuhan, the uncritical media relativist? Among a number of left academics in Canada, McLuhan has been vilified for negating much of what Innis stood for. Therefore, on one side of the ledger there is not now nor has there ever been a Toronto School.

But a compelling argument can be made the other way: The shared concern (accommodating admittedly divergent points of view) for a uniquely important field of study—communications—and an approach to it—historiographical—that has as its institutional epicenter Canada's largest university, now housing both Innis College (established in 1964) and the McLuhan Program in Culture and Technology (originally set up in 1963 by McLuhan as the Centre for Culture and Technology). When regarded inclusively, the Toronto School can be seen as comprising media scholars such as Innis, McLuhan, Havelock, Derrick de Kerckhove, and Robert Logan—all having or having had a physical presence at the University of Toronto—along with anyone anywhere whose work builds on the tradition(s) they embody. For example, Walter Ong, who has done major work on orality and literacy, was a student of McLuhan, and Goody, a Cambridge-based anthropologist who was initially reluctant to see himself as part of the Toronto School after having been perhaps the first to declare its existence, is now comfortable with the affiliation.[21]

The resurrection of Innis's communication studies in light of popular interest in the subject generated by McLuhan, which Carey had undertaken, was expanded on by Kuhns in his book *The Post-industrial Prophets: Interpretations of Technology*.[22] William Kuhns links the work of Innis and McLuhan to a twentieth-century intellectual tradition that assesses, both in a pessimistic and optimistic way, the impact of technology on the natural and social environments and the ways in which technology itself has become an environment. A pantheon of key thinkers is created and examined. It includes, on the pessimistic side, Lewis Mumford, Sigfried Giedion, and Jacques Ellul; and on the optimistic side, Norbert Weiner and Buckminster Fuller. Innis and McLuhan are assessed with respect to the contribution they make to the study of media environments, with Innis leaning toward the critical side of the pantheon and McLuhan associated with the less cautionary more futuristic-oriented thinkers.

During the 1970s, a gradual reassessment of Innis's legacy also began in Canada. At first, it was led by scholars in geography, history, and political economy, whose interests centered on his early work. The decade also saw the establishment of communication studies as an academic discipline, and with it the start of what became over the next several decades a major reevaluation and application of Innisian ideas to communications. In some instances, the beginnings of this project were accompanied by a devaluation of McLuhan, since his work was seen to not represent (occasionally it was regarded as an embarrassment) the directions in which Canadian communication and media studies were supposed to be heading.

An important coming together of scholars in a wide range of fields who had been studying and in some cases applying Innis to a variety of contemporary problems, both economic and media related, occurred in March 1978 in the symposium H. A. Innis: Legacy, Context, Direction, at Simon Fraser University in Burnaby, British Columbia. The proceedings were eventually published.[23]

The symposium featured contributors from a generation who had known and worked with Innis, along with papers by younger scholars appreciative of the relevance of his ideas to their own research interests. The eminent Canadian historian Donald Grant Creighton, who twenty-one years earlier had written the first and to date only personal biography of Innis, gave the keynote address. Among the senior scholars who contributed, Robin Neill, Irene Spry, and Mel Watkins reassessed Innis's staples thesis and his overall legacy to political economy. The lead paper in the communications division was given by Carey, who charted links between Innis and American historical geography. The relationship between Innis and McLuhan was broached by Donald Theall, a former student of both McLuhan and Carpenter, who had also been involved with them in the *Explorations* project.

By the early 1980s, with Innis's rightful place as one of Canada's major inter-disciplinary scholars firmly established, interest in his work in media studies began to trickle south. Carey had already provided the groundwork; Daniel J. Czitrom, Neil Postman, and Joshua Meyrowitz followed with Innisian assess-ments and applications that still remain influential. Their respective projects also resurrected McLuhan. This dual agenda might seem puzzling today, but it must be remembered that throughout the 1970s McLuhan's star waned rapidly (despite his 1977 appearance in Woody Allen's *Annie Hall*) from the supernova status it achieved in the late 1960s. Surprisingly, his death in 1980 attracted relatively little attention. However, in the years that followed, with the hype of his celebrity status now a quaint memory from a more flamboyant decade, his ideas were beginning to be examined more open-mindedly. Today, his stat-ure, although not what it was in the 1960s, is secure, with *Wired* magazine recently declaring him its patron saint.

A key text in initiating the McLuhan-Innis renaissance, if such a term is war-ranted, is Czitrom's *Media and the American Mind: From Morse to McLuhan*.[24] The book adopts an intriguing and effective two-part structure. The first part examines the formative technological and institutional development of three significant communication media in American history: the telegraph, which initiated the electric age; early motion pictures; and broadcast radio. What makes Czitrom's account different from previous assessments of these media is the strong emphasis he puts on popular reactions to their entry into the cultural mainstream.

The second part then looks at three major traditions in communication thought that have influenced American media research. The first is the work of Charles Horton Cooley, John Dewey, and Park, who explored the "holistic nature" of modern media; the second involves the "effects" approach, in which Paul Lazarsfeld looms as the primary figure in a tradition responsible for the prevailing paradigm in contemporary American communication studies; and the third is the historically informed work of Innis and McLuhan that examines the impact of media on social and psychological organization.

Czitrom's appreciation of the "Canadian connection" is unequivocal. His observation that they represent the "most radical and elaborate" legacy to American media theory is cited in the preface to this book. Not surprisingly, he declares his indebtedness to Carey at the outset, but Czitrom's analysis further explores Innis's roots in political economy and his work as part of "a conscious Canadian attack on the burgeoning American cultural and economic hegem-ony in the postwar world."[25] Strong emphasis is placed on the Innis-Veblen connection. Czitrom also tries to identify Innis's philosophical position, which he labels "radical pessimism," and the possibility for a further extension of

Innisian thought is highlighted with a brief application to broadcasting, an area Innis mentions only in passing.

In 1982, Neil Postman entered the domain of extending further various implications of the Innis-McLuhan legacy. *The Disappearance of Childhood* marked his shift from writing primarily about education, to exploring the role of media in contemporary culture through a historically informed perspective. He followed with *Amusing Ourselves to Death, Technopoly: The Surrender of Culture to Technology,* and *Building a Bridge to the Eighteenth Century: How the Past Can Improve Our Future,* thereby becoming one of the most insistent and popular critics of the impact of technology on our time.[26] In *Disappearance of Childhood,* he draws from Carey's lead and takes "as a guide the teachings of Harold Innis," who "stressed that changes in communication technology invariably have three kinds of effects: They alter the structure of interests (the things thought about), the character of symbols (the things thought with), and the nature of the community (the area in which thoughts develop)."[27]

In *Disappearance of Childhood,* Innis and McLuhan receive cobilling given the centrality of the printing press to Postman's argument; according to him, it created the concept of childhood now under siege from today's entertainment media. In Postman's subsequent work, McLuhan receives greater emphasis, since he explored more fully than Innis the electronic media with which Postman has been increasingly concerned. Postman, however, takes a critical stance on contemporary media alien to the McLuhan sources from which he draws, *Gutenberg Galaxy* and *Understanding Media.* Unfortunately, nowhere does Postman cite *Mechanical Bride,* where McLuhan takes a moralistic position that Postman would surely find comparable with his own—for example, *Mechanical Bride*'s contention that modern advertising media are making trivial things seem profound and profound things trivial seems highly consonant with the central argument of *Amusing Ourselves to Death.*

As a critical scholar of media, Postman seems to share an unacknowledged kinship with Innis, but with at least one intriguing difference. Whereas Innis laments the loss of orality (especially dialogue) that is a consequence of modern media monopolies, Postman is more concerned with the way today's electronic media are eclipsing the values of literate thinking (especially reasoned analysis), that characterized the preelectronic print era. While Innis urges us to rediscover the possibilities inherent in the Greek oral tradition, Postman, especially in *Building a Bridge to the Eighteenth Century,* makes a plea for us not to forget what print-based literacy has contributed to culture.

In 1986, after almost a decade of thinking about the relationship between contemporary mass media, especially television, on everyday life, Joshua Meyrowitz published the award-winning *No Sense of Place: The Impact of Electronic Media on Social Behavior.*[28] More than any previous scholar, Meyrowitz was able to cross-fertilize an understanding of communications as a dominant aspect of technologies' influence on contemporary culture with patterns of behavior that characterize the scenarios of everyday life. Two major sources influenced his project: on the media side, McLuhan (and Innis secondarily); on the (micro)social side, Erving Goffman, noted for his study of social behavior in face-to-face "situationist" contexts. Meyrowitz intersects these two disparate traditions in a detailed and compelling analysis that considers everything from gender roles to political image making.

In expanding on and applying the ideas of McLuhan, Meyrowitz invokes and summarizes the work of Innis. When conjoined, their legacies provide him with the mainframe of an approach he calls "medium theory," defined as the "historical and cross-cultural study of the different cultural environments created by different media of communication."[29] Meyrowitz also extends his list of medium theorists to include a number of figures who, as we have seen earlier, are sometimes associated with the so-called Toronto School of communication studies—Carpenter, Goody, Havelock, and Ong.

The term "medium theory" has endured, though not everyone using it subscribes to Meyrowitz's original definition. In the essay "Medium Theory," which was written almost ten years after *No Sense of Place,* he provides a useful expansion of the concept, noting that medium theorists "suggest that each medium invites, allows, encourages, fosters some human actions while discouraging others."[30] The debt here to Innis is clear and made more so in a section "First-Generation Medium Theorists." Meyrowitz declares that there are two, and discusses Innis's work and key concepts along with those of McLuhan. Taken together, their legacies provide us with a research program that as Meyrowitz succinctly points out, allows us to assess "[s]uch variables as the senses that are required to attend to the medium, whether communication is bi-directional or uni-directional, how quickly messages can be disseminated, whether learning how to encode and decode the medium is difficult or simple, how many people can attend to the same message at the same moment and [how] such variables influence the medium's use and its social, political, and psychological impact."[31]

The 1990s saw various Innis commentaries emerge in Canada in the years leading up to and following the 1994 centenary of his birth. An overture of sorts to these discussions was set in 1984 with the publication of Arthur Kroker's influential *Technology and the Canadian Mind: Innis, McLuhan, Grant.*[32] What makes Kroker's study significant is that it is more than a basic appraisal of the legacies of three unconventional north-of-the-border scholars. He attempts to see Innis, McLuhan, and the less well known (outside of Canada) George Grant (a philosopher) as sharing a distinctly Canadian discourse on technology, resulting from the country's marginality to the United States. This discourse is also linked to an ethos that is a mix of the country's traditional European past and a postmodern high-tech future; it contrasts markedly, according to Kroker, with the "present mindedness" of the United States.

This ethos not only underscores the work of the three principal figures Kroker assesses, he discerns it in the Canadian art, literature, and even architecture—for example, in the tallest free-standing structure (Canadians claim building) in the world, the Canadian National Tower, which dominates the cityscape of Toronto, an architectural idea from the past (obelisk, church spire) embraces a state-of-the-art telecommunications facility that exudes corporate power. Out of the secure past and uncertain future of the country emerged these three distinct yet related thinkers whose forte was assessing the relationship between technology and culture. McLuhan's work—but not his guarded personal sentiments—expresses optimism; Grant presents us with a darker more brooding vision; and, as Kroker perceptively notes,

> [i]f McLuhan and Grant are the polar opposites of the Canadian mind, this can only mean that their must be a *third perspective* in the Canadian discourse on technology which mediates technological humanism with technological dependency. And that is the critical perspective of *technological realism*, whose leading advocate is the political economist, Harold A. Innis. Grant might write a tragic "lament" and McLuhan might privilege the utopian possibilities of technology, but Innis' ideal was always attaining "balance and proportion" between the competing claims of empire (power) and culture (history).[33]

Although chronologically Innis is the earliest of the three sages assessed in *Technology and the Canadian Mind*, Kroker deals with him last. As in the assessment by Carey (who is not cited), Innis is privileged over McLuhan. He is seen as both a "shaman" and a "pragmatic realist" who more than the other two understood his country in relation to the successive waves of imperial influence it has experienced—French, British, and American. Such marginal status can yield unique insights into the conditions that render it marginal, and in Innis's case this led him to an appraisal of the dynamics of Western civilization, monopolies, and the mechanization of culture. As Kroker shows, the weight of such a daunting program compelled Innis to humor and at times sarcasm, which only served to add more insight to his critique.

Unlike most Innis commentators before him, Kroker makes reference to essays in *Changing Concepts of Time,* especially "The Strategy of Culture" and "Military Implications of the American Constitution." Margaret Atwood's notion that survival is the central symbol in Canadian culture is also incorporated into his analysis, as are theoretical elements in Innis's writing that Kroker links to a venerable south-of-the-border, scholarly tradition, "Innis was the last and best of the Chicago School thinkers."[34] McLuhan espouses the same view.

Both he and Kroker argue that Park was a major influence on Innis, a contention Carey strongly disputes. No matter, Kroker's overall assessment of Innis as
a Canadian scholar, both in the world and of it, is compelling and provides
sustenance for his own subsequent critique of technology in the postmodern
world.[35]

Canadian media culture has always been blessed with a strong documentary
film tradition through the auspices of the National Film Board, the Canadian
Broadcasting Corporation, and individuals inspired by the work that has ema-
nated from these institutions. In 1990, Alison Beale, a Simon Fraser University
professor of communication, wrote and directed the documentary *Harold Innis:
Patterns in Communication*. It incorporates archival film footage and photographs, letters, interviews with sons Donald and Hugh, and a host of insightful
commentators. Throughout the documentary, the voice of Innis is rendered
by an actor. Unfortunately, there seems to be no archival recording on disk,
tape, or film of Innis speaking.[36]

On a more conventional scholarly front, 1990 also saw the release of Graeme
Patterson's *History and Communications: Harold Innis, Marshall McLuhan, and the
Interpretation of History*.[37] Patterson locates Innis's work in relation to distinctively Canadian traditions of historiography. He provides a thorough analysis
of its philosophical underpinnings, especially in light of the materialist–idealist
debate. A strong argument is also presented in favor of logical continuity
between the early and later Innis—Innis's concept of communication is seen
as an outgrowth of his economic studies of transport and understanding of the
nature and function of commodities. It appears that Patterson's goal here is to
allay some of the bewilderment among Canadian historians regarding where
Innis went in his later writings and why. Another concern of the book is to
show the degree to which McLuhan might have been influenced by Innis, and
even though the argument is convincing, some McLuhan interpreters might
feel that Patterson attributes more influence than is warranted.

Besides the Innis discussions that took place in Canada and the United States
at this time, Australian communication scholars were finding his work relevant
to some of their concerns. In 1993, *Continuum: The Australian Journal of Media
and Culture* published a special issue, "Dependency/Space/Policy: A Dialogue
with Harold A. Innis." Two notable contributions are Brian Shoesmith's
"Introduction to Innis' 'History of Communication,'" and Hart Cohen's
"Margins at the Centre: Innis' Concept of Bias and the Development of
Aboriginal Media." The first is a brief account of Innis's unpublished "History
of Communications" manuscript, followed by an excerpt from it titled "Printing in China in the 19th and 20th Century"; the second explores the encounter between a culture with a rich oral tradition and modern electronic media.[38]

In celebration of the centenary of Innis birth in 1994, various conferences were held in Montreal, Toronto, and Vancouver. Two commemorative volumes eventually resulted. Daniel Drache, a political economist at Toronto's York University, edited a collection of Innis writings titled *Staples, Markets, and Cultural Change: Harold Innis.*[39] The title suggests a dominant political economy slant, and the introduction by Drache is indeed a comprehensive and significant assessment of Innis's work in this area. However, the book is in effect a highly representative Innis reader containing important selections from both his early and later periods.

The Innis centenary also inspired an anthology of commentaries on and extensions of his work. Edited by Charles R. Acland and William J. Buxton, two communication studies faculty from Concordia University in Montreal, *Harold Innis in the New Century: Reflections and Refractions* is a diverse and comprehensive essay collection.[40] In their introduction, Buxton and Acland provide an insightful overview of previous Innis assessments, both positive and critical. The first part then continues the appraisal with the help of veteran commentators such as Carey and Irene Spry (who worked with Innis), along with several newer voices. The second part looks at issues relevant to an Innisian approach to which he either gave short shrift or overlooked completely. The third part is a response to his work by a number of scholars inspired by the contemporary cultural studies project.

The second half of the 1990s in Canada saw numerous applications of Innisian concepts to the analysis of communication and culture. Most of these studies emphasized scenarios that were historically recent. A notable exception is the work of Ronald Deibert, a professor of political science at the University of Toronto. In the major undertaking *Parchment, Printing, and Hypermedia: Communication in World Order Transformation,* he uses a perspective on medium theory indebted to Innis and McLuhan (also to Mumford and Fernand Braudel) to assess the influence communication media have exerted on world order transformation in three epochs: the Middle Ages, through the Catholic Church's use of the parchment codex; the transition to modernity fostered by the printing press; and finally, informed by these case studies, he looks at the global role of hypermedia in the transformation to today's postmodern, postindustrial information age.[41]

Deibert effectively uses medium theory to develop what he calls an "ecological holist" approach that allows him to expand the mandate of his primary field of study, international relations. The book makes a strong case for the study of communications in the past informing the present in areas such as the transnationalization of production and finance (anticipated in the Catholic Church's corporate hold on Europe during the Middle Ages) and the shifts occurring in global politics and policy making that have occurred in the transition from the modern to the postmodern hypermedia world of digital technology, the Internet, and high-resolution satellite imaging.

By the start of the new millennium, Innis's stature was secure nationally, with worldwide interest on the rise. His work, along with McLuhan's, has often been regarded as virtually synonymous with communication thought in Canada. But there were others. In *Canadian Communication Thought: Ten Foundational Writers,* media scholar Robert E. Babe endeavors to assess this tradition.[42] Innis and McLuhan receive coverage, of course, but so do eight additional figures; the work of some of them is indebted to Innis and McLuhan, while others, such as the renowned literary critic Northrop Frye, have pursued separate lines of inquiry.

The project was inspired by Carey's now classic 1967 essay on Innis and McLuhan. Babe is equally versed in political economy and media studies and the book brings both dimensions to an assessment of Innis's legacy. New light is shed on Innis's early work on the Canadian Pacific Railway, and several Innisian notions are compared with those of Adam Smith—not only with reference to his *Inquiry into the Nature and Causes of the Wealth of Nations,* but also to the much neglected but equally important (when considering communication processes) *Theory of Moral Sentiments.*[43] The chapter ends with some insightful suggestions on the applications of Innisian thought to digital media in the contemporary world.

Finally, as we now move further into the information age and the dramatic consequences of the computer, it becomes increasingly obvious that this technology shares ways of structuring information with the various earlier forms of communication studied by Innis. Computer technology, depending on its application, can manifest elements of an oral tradition in the dialogue that emerges in the elective networks and nonlocalized interest groups that form through the Internet; it can evidence a time-bias in terms of the preservation and almost ritual access to knowledge that would be otherwise lost; a space-bias can also be observed in the computer's ability to disseminate same-source information globally in the manner of a mass medium; and despite what its defenders claim, it can lead to various monopolies of knowledge, corporate and communal.

Innis may have written decades prior to the emergence of the information age, but his acute understanding of the interaction between communication and culture, from antiquity to modernity, has ongoing relevance to our understanding of it in the newly minted history of the twenty-first century.

NOTES

1. For an assessment of the significance of Marshall McLuhan's *The Mechanical Bride: Folklore of Industrial Man* (Boston: Beacon, 1967), see Paul Heyer, *Communications and History: Theories of Media, Knowledge, and Civilization* (Westport, Conn.: Greenwood, 1988).

2. From an interview in the video documentary *Harold Innis: Patterns in Communication,* prod. and dir. Alison Beale, 52 min., 1990, videocassette.

3. Harold A. Innis, *The Bias of Communication* (1951; reprint, with an introduction by Paul Heyer and David Crowley, Toronto: University of Toronto Press, 1995).

4. See Matie Molinaro, Corinne McLuhan, and William Toye, eds., *The Letters of Marshall McLuhan* (New York: Oxford University Press, 1987).

5. In Molinaro, McLuhan, and Toye, *Letters of Marshall McLuhan,* 448.

6. Marshall McLuhan, *The Gutenberg Galaxy: The Making of a Typographic Man* (New York: Signet, 1969), 65; Innis is also cited in the bibliography of Marshall McLuhan, *Understanding Media: The Extensions of Man* (New York: Signet, 1964).

7. Marshall McLuhan, foreword to *Empire and Communications,* by Harold A. Innis (1950; reprint, Toronto: University of Toronto Press, 1975), ix.

8. Anne Innis Dagg, interview with the author, Waterloo, Ontario, August 15, 2002.

9. Edmund Carpenter, "That Not So Silent Sea," in *The Virtual McLuhan,* by Donald F. Theall (Montreal: McGill-Queen's University Press, 2001), 248–250.

10. Carpenter, "That Not So Silent Sea," 238–239.

11. John Houseman, *Entertainers and the Entertained* (New York: Simon and Schuster, 1986).

12. Houseman, *Entertainers and the Entertained,* 291.

13. Houseman, *Entertainers and the Entertained,* 292.

14. James W. Carvey, "Harold Adams Innis and Marshall McLuhan," *The Antioch Review* 27, no. 1 (Spring 1967).

15. James W. Carey, "Space, Time, and Communications: A Tribute to Harold Innis," in *Communication As Culture: Essays on Media and Society,* by James W. Carey (Boston: Unwin Hyman, 1989), 142.

16. James W. Carey, "Harold Adams Innis and Marshall McLuhan," in *McLuhan Pro and Con,* ed. Raymond Rosenthal (Baltimore, Md.: Penguin, 1969), 281.

17. James W. Carey, *Communication As Culture: Essays on Media and Society* (Boston: Unwin Hyman, 1989).

18. Jack Goody, *Literacy in Traditional Societies* (Cambridge: Cambridge University Press, 1968).

19. Jack Goody, *The Domestication of the Savage Mind* (Cambridge: Cambridge University Press, 1977); Jack Goody, *The Logic of Writing and the Organization of Society* (Cambridge: Cambridge University Press, 1986).

20. Derrick de Kerckhove, "McLuhan and the Toronto School of Communication," *Canadian Journal of Communication* 14, nos. 4–5 (December 1989): 73.

21. Jack Goody, personal conversation with the author, Vancouver, British Columbia, May 1994.

22. William Kuhns, *The Post-industrial Prophets: Interpretations of Technology* (New York: Weybright and Talley, 1971).

23. William Melody, Liora Salter, and Paul Heyer, *Culture, Communication, and Dependency: The Tradition of H. A. Innis* (Norwood, N.J.: Ablex, 1981).

24. Daniel J. Czitrom, *Media and the American Mind: From Morse to McLuhan* (Chapel Hill: University of North Carolina Press, 1982).

25. Czitrom, *Media and the American Mind,* 147.

26. Neil Postman, *The Disappearance of Childhood* (New York: Laurel, 1984); Neil Postman, *Amusing Ourselves to Death* (New York: Penguin, 1986); Neil Postman, *Technopoly: The*

Surrender of Culture to Technology (New York: Knopf, 1992); Neil Postman, *Building a Bridge to the Eighteenth Century: How the Past Can Improve Our Future* (New York: Knopf, 1999).

27. Postman, *Disappearance of Childhood*, 23.

28. Joshua Meyrowitz, *No Sense of Place: The Impact of Electronic Media on Social Behavior* (New York: Oxford University Press, 1986).

29. Meyrowitz, *No Sense of Place*, 16.

30. Joshua Meyrowitz, "Medium Theory," in *Communication Theory Today*, ed. David Crowley and David Mitchell (Stanford, Calif.: Stanford University Press, 1994), 71.

31. Meyrowitz, "Medium Theory," 50.

32. Arthur Kroker, *Technology and the Canadian Mind: Innis, McLuhan, Grant* (Montreal: New World Perspectives, 1984).

33. Kroker, *Technology and the Canadian Mind*, 15.

34. Kroker, *Technology and the Canadian Mind*, 106.

35. For example, see Arthur Kroker and Marilouise Kroker, eds., *The Panic Encyclopedia: The Definitive Guide to the Postmodern Scene* (Montreal: New World Perspectives, 1989); Arthur Kroker and Marilouise Kroker, *Ideology and Power in the Age of Lenin in Ruins* (New York: St. Martin's, 1991).

36. Research for this book has similarly failed to discover any voice recording of Innis.

37. Graeme Patterson, *History and Communications: Harold Innis, Marshall McLuhan, and the Interpretation of History* (Toronto: University of Toronto Press, 1990).

38. Brian Shoesmith, "Introduction to Innis' 'History of Communication,'" *Continuum: The Australian Journal of Media and Culture* 7, no. 1 (1993): 121–131; Hart Cohen, "Margins at the Centre: Innis' Concept of Bias to the Development of Aboriginal Media," *Continuum: The Australian Journal of Media and Culture* 7, no. 1 (1993): 105–120.

39. Daniel Drache, ed., *Staples, Markets, and Cultural Change: Harold Innis* (Montreal: McGill-Queen's University Press, 1995).

40. Charles R. Acland and William J. Buxton, eds., *Harold Innis in the New Century: Reflections and Refractions* (Montreal: McGill-Queens University Press, 1995).

41. Ronald Deibert, *Parchment, Printing, and Hypermedia: Communication in World Order Transformation* (New York: Columbia University Press, 1997). See also Lewis Mumford, *Technics and Civilization* (New York: Harcourt, Brace, 1934); Fernand Braudel, *La Méditerranée at le monde méditerranée à l'époque de Philippe II* (Paris: Librairie Armand Colin, 1949).

42. Robert E. Babe, *Canadian Communication Thought: Ten Foundational Writers* (Toronto: University of Toronto Press, 2000).

43. Adam Smith, *Inquiry into the Nature and Causes of the Wealth of Nations* (1776; reprint, Buffalo, N.Y.: Prometheus, 1991); Adam Smith, *The Theory of Moral Sentiments* (1759; reprint, Amherst, N.Y.: Prometheus, 2000).

Epilogue

Improvements in communication have weakened the possibility of sustained thought when it has become most necessary.

—Harold A. Innis

There is no finer sight than that of the intelligence at grips with a reality that transcends it.

—Albert Camus

Rightly or wrongly, Marshall McLuhan once described his work as a footnote to Innis. It would not be an exaggeration to suggest that a good deal of Innis commentary could be construed as a footnote to James Carey's 1967 essay. Carey showed many of us the broad contours and relevance of Innis's communication thought; he also suggested that there was even more to the legacy than could be accommodated in his appraisal. Far from being the last word on Innis, Carey's essay is, in effect, the first full-blown invitation to explore further the implications of Innis's later writings. The preceding pages can in some sense be seen as an acceptance of that invitation.

In his later work, Innis was certainly not a historian's historian. His conceptual framework eschewed detailed analysis in favor of broad generalizations that encompass entire epochs. He also did not set out to do history for its own sake, but instead used the past to measure the present. Michel Foucault, whose examination of pattern and power in history has several points in common with Innis—such as epochal divisions having distinct configurations of power and knowledge—has referred to his own approach as a "history of the present." The same label could be applied to Innis. And, political economist that Innis was until the end, material factors, such as staple resources and transportation and communication technologies, are accorded a dominant role in historical transformation.

He brought to his work a dialectical understanding of change, whereby new media challenge old, and in the resulting collision of communication and culture, social formations—sometimes entire civilizations—rise and fall. In assessing this push and pull, he employed a series of revealing concepts: the oral tradition, time-bias and space-bias, monopolies of knowledge, and the mechanization of culture. Granted, his application of these concepts is not always convincing, as several critics have pointed out—for example, I find his understanding of orality wanting on several points, given its limited anthropological scope and overreliance on the early Greek cultural tradition as a case study. But with Innis the whole is always greater than the sum of its parts. His vision is *programmatic*. Josh Meyrowitz and Ronald Deibert refer to it as medium theory. I sometimes use the term "communications history." No matter, it is first and foremost an approach (dare I say paradigm?), and secondarily a series of hypotheses.

Unlike McLuhan, who would eventually regard his avowedly tentative "probes" as dogma, intellectual honesty compelled Innis to view his own formulations as provisional, as indicated in the exchange with Gordon Childe discussed in chapter 2. Innis's communication project remained incomplete and probably would have stayed that way even if he had lived another ten years because it is inherently open-ended—the sketch map for a new scholarly subcontinent that invites further exploration rather than closure. Friedrich Nietzsche once observed, and Michel Foucault following him, that those who wish to honor their work should challenge and extend it, not dwell on interpretations. Most likely Innis would have felt the same way.

The man himself emerges as an intense, driven scholar who was also endowed with a wry sense of humor. Yes, Innis curried administrative favor, as Eric Havelock has noted, but it is clear that he never compromised his critical scholarly ideals when he did. There is also a darkness in his later writings—the "radical pessimism" Daniel J. Czitrom alludes to—laced with touches of skepticism. Innis seems to imply that monopolies of knowledge are an inevitable aspect of historical formation and he is never deluded, as he felt some of his colleagues were, by false optimism regarding the possibilities of radical change.

Nevertheless, his critique of those monopolies is unyielding, even though his efforts on behalf of policy, such as in educational reform, were usually deemed impractical and rarely accepted. For me, Innis embodies qualities that one of his contemporaries, Albert Camus, attributes to the modern tragic hero: Condemned to both freedom and an absurd world, he lives without hope, but also without resignation, in a state of conscious revolt against the inequities of that world. In Innis's case, that revolt yielded a new way of understanding both history and history in the making.

Harold A. Innis's "History of Communications" Manuscript

William J. Buxton

During the last dozen years of his life, Harold A. Innis assembled a massive set of writings entitled "A History of Communications: An Incomplete and Unrevised Manuscript." Overall, it is around fourteen hundred pages in length, with a time span running from ancient India and China (circa 1500 B.C.) to the twentieth century, with the eighteenth and nineteenth centuries receiving particular attention. In addition, Innis produced around one thousand pages of manuscript covering in more detail the development of communications in antiquity. Very likely, this material was intended to comprise the first part of the manuscript, but was never transferred into typewritten form. It is for good reason that Innis gave the document the subtitle "An Incomplete and Unrevised Manuscript"! Copies of the manuscript can be found at the University of Toronto Archives, at the National Archives in Ottawa, and (in microfiche form) at the McLennan Library of McGill University.

It is not entirely clear when Innis produced the manuscript or what he intended to do with it. Robin Neill claims that Innis had completed it by 1945 and drew on it in preparing "the addresses and articles that *were* published between 1945 and 1952."[1] In effect, Neill views the document as a massive repository of factual data that Innis then fashioned into his published work by making "its interpretive insights more explicit." Neill's assessment of the manuscript reflects the conventional wisdom about it. The document has largely been viewed as an extensive collection of reading notes lacking the theoretical glosses that punctuate Innis's published writings on the same general subject.

Given that this view of the manuscript has gained widespread acceptance, scholars have largely steered clear of the document when examining Innis's communications work, preferring instead to rely on his published work. More-over, in view of its bulk, coupled with its reputation as little more than a mas-sive assemblage of factual material, none of the efforts to publish it have ever reached fruition.[2]

My research on the writing and content of the document suggests that a reassessment of its nature and significance is in order. Archival sources on Innis's activities during the postwar period reveal that Innis's primary research on the history of communications continued well after 1945, suggesting that the large document was actually assembled at a later date. Specifically, Innis received a small grant from the Rockefeller Foundation to undertake research on "the problems of paper production in France and the relationship to the general subject of communications" in London and Paris during the summer of 1948. During the spring of that same year, he had been invited to deliver the Beit Lectures at Oxford University, the Stamp Lecture at the University of London, and the Cust Lecture at the University of Nottingham. In all likeli-hood, Innis took advantage of his lecture invitations to continue his research on the history of communications. Given that chapters VI, VII, and VIII of "History of Communications" contain a good deal of material on paper pro-duction in France, one can conclude that Innis was still in the process of pre-paring the document between 1948 and his death in 1952.

That Innis had planned to do further research after his visit to Paris and Lon-don in 1948 was evident in his intention, conveyed to the Rockefeller Foun-dation in 1948, to "take a leave of absence in a year or two . . . to visit India and other countries in the east . . . to explore developments in the work on communication and in particular the place of oral communication." These items suggest that Innis produced revised drafts of a number of chapters of "History of Communications" after 1948, and may have then written by hand a lengthy manuscript on communication in antiquity that he intended to include as the first three chapters of the final version of the already bulky docu-ment. Because of his heavy obligations during the following two years (he was the dean of the Faculty of Graduate Studies at the University of Toronto and a member of the Royal Commission on Transportation), he was not able to visit India and other Asian countries to undertake research on the oral tradition. However, both "History of Communications" and the section in *The Idea File of Harold Adams Innis* for the years 1949 and 1950 include numerous references to patterns of communication in various parts of Asian countries during antiq-uity.[3] This provides a good indication that he was able to follow through on his research plan, using available sources rather than going abroad. Hence, one can safely conclude that the material presented in "History of Communica-tions" was based on fresh research conducted after Innis's Beit Lectures at Oxford in 1948, which provided the basis for *Empire and Communications*.

If it indeed was the case that the production of "History of Communications" was an ongoing process during the last dozen years of Innis's life, then one must also reexamine the relationship between the manuscript and his published writings on communications of the late 1940s and early 1950s. It might very well be the case that the document had its own integrity and represented a body of work that was emerging in parallel fashion to that of his published work. To be sure, Innis likely drew on this set of writings for his other published writings. But as the evidence suggests, Innis worked continually on this document until his death and fully intended to revise it and see it through to publication.

It would also appear that the work was continuous with both *Political Economy and the Modern State* and *Empire and Communications.*⁴ Like the latter work, it was conceived as a full-scale study of civilization, in the tradition of such authors as Oswald Spengler, Arnold Toynbee, Alfred Kroeber, and Pitirim Sorokin. However, there is some evidence that "History of Communications" was rooted in a framework that went beyond the "highly integrated and global one" that was deployed in *Political Economy and the Modern State* and further refined in *Empire and Communications.* Innis sought an alternative to the mainstream of political history, advocating rather a "total history" that placed an emphasis on tracing the interplay of economic, cultural, social, and geographical factors in determining the course of civilizational development. In undertaking this kind of history, emphasis was placed not only on conjunctural factors, but also on cycles and *longues durées* (i.e., epochs). Such considerations had not only marked both the work of both Lucien Febvre and Marc Bloch, his cofounder of the *Annales* journal, but also in the work of the rising star of the school, Fernand Braudel, who had just published his monumental study of the civilization that surrounded the Mediterranean Sea.⁵ What this suggests is that Innis sought to produce a major work along the lines of those monumental studies produced by these *Annales* scholars.

While these issues certainly can be found in his writings on communications, particularly in *Empire and Communications,* in "History of Communications" they are much more sharply focused in terms of political organization as it related to monopolies of control over territory through force, means of communication, and ideas. In all likelihood, Innis was moving toward an integrative interpretive framework for the work, along the lines of what he had previously developed in his major works such as *The Fur Trade in Canada, The Cod Fisheries: The History of an International Economy,* and *Empire and Communications.* In the same way that his framework of analysis in each of his previous major works built on that of its immediate predecessor, "History of Communications" was built on what he had developed earlier in *Empire and Communica-*

tions, in *The Bias of Communication,* and in *Political Economy and the Modern State.*[6]

If Innis had lived longer, he may very well have seen the work through to completion. It would have been a massive volume with enormous historical sweep, making particular claims about the development of states and civilizations from antiquity to modernity. Since the project was cut short by Innis's untimely death, what we are left with is a large and unruly assemblage of materials whose underlying conceptual framework is only intermittently evident. However, by drawing on the themes outlined in his Paris talk, by the notions expressed in his later lectures and notes, and by other contemporaneous writings, one can begin to make sense of what the document is about.

Despite its title, the manuscript is not about the history of communications taken *tout court;* it deals with the history of printing and publishing from around the second century B.C. (with the coming of paper in China) to the twentieth century. In typical Innisian fashion, great attention is given to the material aspects of printing, including not only the advances in typemaking and typesetting, but also in the development of paper and ink. The overall narrative, however, is not simply one of technological advance. Innis gives particular attention to the relationship between printing and monopolies of knowledge and power as they shifted and developed over time. As William Christian so aptly notes, "For Innis the most problematic element of the modern world was mechanization and the associated battery of beliefs and practices that mechanization called forth. If he were to point to one salient cause of the character of modern civilization, it would be the printing press."[7] This suggests that "History of Communications" is really about modernity, as attendant on the development of paper and printing.

The material is presented chronologically, with the various chapters covering developments over the course of succeeding centuries within specific national contexts. This suggests that Innis envisioned history as consisting of a series of interconnected *longues durées,* each having particular defining characteristics. Overall, the work consists of eight large sections (ranging in size from forty to three hundred pages), accompanied by twelve fragments and short treatments (ranging in size from three to nineteen pages). The first five large sections bear chapter numbers from "IV" to "VIII." The last three large sections appear to correspond to chapters, given their themes and order, but do not bear chapter numbers. This suggests that Innis was still in the process of blocking out the work into specific chapters when he died. That the first chapter is listed as "Chapter IV: The Coming of Paper" suggests that he planned to include three chapters dealing with earlier developments. The fragments at the end of the material suggest that he wished to carry through the analysis into the twentieth century, making particular reference to newspapers.

A lengthy initial chapter on the coming of paper is followed by three fragments dealing with particular themes related to the Middle Ages, namely on classical literature, Geoffrey Chaucer, and the thirteenth century. The work then picks up with "Chapter V: Printing in the Fifteenth Century." The chapters that follow address similar themes in relation to particular centuries, moving from the sixteenth to the nineteenth centuries. The final part of the work breaks down into a series of fragments again. This suggests that Innis planned to integrate some of them into the body of the text (the Frankfurt Bookfair) and to continue his analysis into the twentieth century (Newspaper Press after 1900). The presence of two short excerpts on China in the nineteenth and twentieth centuries indicates that he planned to compare outcomes between China and the West.

What follows is an overview of the manuscript's content, accompanied by the number of pages for each item. For the untitled treatments, the first few words of each have been used to indicate the piece in question:

Chapter IV, "The Coming of Paper"   96 pp.
(nt) "Classical Literature . . ."   18 pp.
(nt) "Within the middle of the 13th Century . . ."   9 pp.
(nt) "Chaucer wrote for . . ."   6 pp.
Chapter V, "Printing in the 15th Century"   43 pp.
(nt) "The Fifteenth Century saw . . ."   6 pp.
Chapter VI, "The Paper and Printing Industries in the 16th Century"   121 pp.
Chapter VII, "The Paper and Printing Industries in the 17th Century"   101 pp.
Chapter VIII, "The Paper and Printing Industries in the 18th Century"   307 pp.
"Paper and Printing in the 19th Century"   161 pp.
"Printing Industry in Britain in the 19th Century"   180 pp.
(addendum)   5 pp.
(nt) "A newspaper is . . ."   18 pp.
"The American Printing Industry in the 19th Century"   262 pp.
(nt) "After the Revolution . . ."   12 pp.
"Newspaper Press before 1900"   12 pp.
"Newspaper Press after 1900"   19 pp.
"Frankfurt Bookfair"   16 pp.
"Printing in China in the 19th Century"   3 pp.
"Printing in China in the 20th Century"   8 pp.

At a first glance, the manuscript covers much of the same ground as *Empire and Communications* and *Bias of Communication*. However, the chapter titles belie what the manuscript actually covers. Even though one finds at least some discussion of paper and printing in each chapter, these subjects have a tendency to fade into the background, giving way to lengthy treatments of such issues as patronage, religion, propaganda, public opinion, education, and war. While these topics figure in his other major writings, they are dealt with in much greater detail and with finer nuance in "History of Communications."

As commentators have been at pains to emphasize, the manuscript largely consists of densely packed factual material and is quite lacking in the occasional theoretical glosses that accompany his other writings on the history of communications. This is not entirely true. Indeed, the document can best be viewed as a set of writings in various stages of development. Some, to be sure, are little more than reading notes. But others are quite well developed and carefully theorized. For instance, "Chapter V: Printing in the 15th Century" has a great deal to say about the significance of printing for the broader social order. Unlike some of the other sprawling chapters, this one is quite short (forty-three pages), is carefully footnoted, and has extensive discussion of how print was related to broader processes of social change. Innis notes, for instance that "[r]eliance on manuscripts limited material to a few individuals. Printing rescued men from the schools. With dependence on manuscripts, reason was outraged, humanity oppressed, and checked by blood and flames."[8] He concludes with the assessment that "[t]he introduction of printing marked the beginning of the long struggle between a civilization based on writing and vellum and a civilization based on paper and the printing press. The spread of commerce from Flanders and Venice brought a revival of cursive writing, the introduction of lay schools, the use of paper and the decline of Latin with the rise of the vernacular."[9]

In much of the manuscript, to be sure, the implications of what Innis is discussing are not made nearly as explicit. Nevertheless, it is evident from the way in which the material has been assembled and periodicized, and by the interconnected set of themes that recur, that the work represents much more than simply an extended compilation of reading notes. Giving shape and meaning to the data in question was a framework of analysis that permitted Innis not only to trace recurring patterns over time, but also to juxtapose developments occurring over space. In effect, the work is implicitly informed by a comparative-historical framework, a mode of analysis that was less consistently adhered to in his other major writings.

In carrying out this analysis, Innis effectively emphasized both material and ideational factors. With regard to the former, for instance, he gave close attention to the material conditions that made the writing and the preparation of texts possible. This led him to examine the institution of patronage and how it was linked to authorship, censorship, and the production of texts. He notes, for instance, that in Elizabethan England (in the late sixteenth century) "uncertainty of patronage produced uneasiness and discontent among writers."[10] Monasteries had ceased their support, and what was offered by the court and patrons was arbitrary and undependable. Within *Empire and Communications,* this subject does not even appear in the index. However, in "History of Communications" Innis returns to this topic time and time again.

At various points in the manuscript, Innis uses a materialist analysis that is almost Marxian in its orientation, focusing on questions of class, power, and struggle. This calls into question the common claim that these sorts of issues were ignored in his political economical analysis. This orientation is particularly evident in chapter VI, which deals with printing in the sixteenth century. In this regard, Innis offers a detailed and nuanced analysis of the labor struggles within the paper industry in France, focusing on how the *compagnons* strata (likely journeymen) defended their rights against the masters and the municipalities, complaining of "inadequate work," decline in wages, and objectives to "pain, vin et pitance."[11] The point of Innis's analysis, in this case, is to better understand the broader shifts in the production of books (such as the division of labor worked out between Paris and Lyons) attendant on the way in which the labor disputes were ultimately resolved.

Innis complemented this materialist form of analysis with one that emphasized more ideational factors. Such a tendency represented a departure from the kind of approach for which he has become known, namely one that focuses on concrete factors such as staples or media technology and their effects. The attention he gives to the importance of ideas and values in "History of Communications" might be interpreted as his recognition of the limitations inherent in the materialist approach, perhaps as a result of his participation in the "Values Seminar" at the University of Toronto, held in the spring of 1949. In any event, this concern was evident in his inclusion of a good deal of contemporary literary material that reflexively addressed how people of the day viewed the development of media. Such items go a long way toward dispelling the view that Innis had little sensitivity to literary and cultural matters, but was obsessed with broader structural patterns. For example, in order to make a point about the importance of rags for the development of paper, he quotes the following lines from a poem of the day:

> From linen rags good paper doth derive
> The first trade keeps the second trade alive.[12]

There is likely more to Innis's inclusion of excerpts from poems such as these than his desire to add a bit a zest to his sometimes dry prose. Consistent with his interest in examining the emergence of public opinion, he showed a consistent interest in trying to reveal what people *thought* about the important issues of the day. This practice is particularly evident in Innis's discussion of how various writers criticized state control of printing in the early seventeenth century. For instance, Innis includes an extensive excerpt from scene five of Ben Jonson's *The Staple of News* (an Innisian title if there ever was one!), noting that this work "reflected a general opinion toward the development of new books."[13]

This concern with reception and public opinion was also reflected in the emphasis that Innis gives to key individuals in the process of modernization. This stood in stark contrast to *Empire and Communications,* in which central figures in the history of printing and publishing are mentioned only in passing. For instance, while Innis writes all of one line on the contributions of Desider- ius Erasmus in *Empire and Communications,* in "History of Communications," the Dutch-born thinker appears frequently in the body of the text, most nota- bly in chapter VI. Innis provides a detailed account of Erasmus's views about the importance of books for scholarship, underscoring how his ideas helped shift the course of history.[14] Elsewhere, summing up a detailed discussion of the thoughts and activities of numerous thinkers, Innis states that "Montaigne and Machiavelli produced the greatest effect upon the age and with Rabelais were the only writers of the sixteenth century read continuously later."[15] What attracted Innis to thinkers such as these was their ability to challenge prevailing notions about reason and knowledge and to change the way that people thought about the way that power was exercised. Along the same lines, Martin Luther, as Innis points out, provided a key linkage between publication and the Reformation.

It should be evident that not only can "History of Communications" be viewed as a project with its own integrity, but that it also contains insights not to be found in his other writings on communications. Yet, as we have seen, it has been virtually ignored. The lack of attention given to the document is con- sistent with a general lack of understanding about Innis's life and work. We have little idea of exactly what Innis wrote over his lifetime, when they were written, or in what circumstances. Indeed, it is not even entirely clear when he embarked on his so-called turn toward communications, and how the massive "History of Communications" document figured into his later work. One does not know, for instance, whether the work was intended to be revised for publication, or whether it was more of a repository of thoughts and material that was meant to be drawn on for publication in discrete bits.

What is at stake is the fact that our understanding of Innis's work has largely emerged in the absence of what could very well have been his most insightful statement about how media have emerged and developed. This would suggest that our collective memory of Innis's thought is (in line with Innis's own mode of analysis) a highly biased one rooted in a particular monopoly of knowledge that has become entrenched. In making the framework, scope, and content of the document better known, it is hoped that one can correct some of this bias and shed light on what Tom Cooper has so aptly described as "the unknown Innis."[16]

NOTES

1. Robin Neill, *A New Theory of Value: The Canadian Economics of H. A. Innis* (Toronto: University of Toronto Press, 1972), 95. Most of these writings can be found in three volumes: *Empire and Communications* (1950; reprint, with a foreword by Marshall McLuhan, Toronto: University of Toronto Press, 1975); *The Bias of Communication* (1951; reprint, with an introduction by Paul Heyer and David Crowley, Toronto: University of Toronto Press, 1995); and *Changing Concepts of Time* (1952; reprint, with a foreword by James W. Carey, Boulder, Colo.: Rowman & Littlefield, 2003). Two essays, however, were not included in these collections: "The English Press in the Nineteenth Century: An Economic Approach," *University of Toronto Quarterly* 15 (1945): 37–53, and "The Newspaper in Economic Development," *Journal of Economic History* 2/s (1942): 1–33.

2. See William J. Buxton, "The Bias against Communication: On the Neglect and Non-publication of the 'Incomplete and Unrevised Manuscript' of Harold Adams Innis," *Canadian Journal of Communication* 26, nos. 2–3 (2001).

3. Harold A. Innis, *The Idea File of Harold Adams Innis,* ed. William Christian (Toronto: University of Toronto Press, 1980).

4. Harold A. Innis, *Political Economy and the Modern State* (Toronto: University of Toronto Press, 1946).

5. Fernand Braudel, *La Méditerranée et le monde méditerranée à l' époque de Philippe II* (Paris: Librairie Armand Colin, 1949).

6. Harold A. Innis, *The Fur Trade in Canada* (1930; reprint, New Haven, Conn.: Yale University Press, 1962); Harold A. Innis, *The Cod Fisheries: The History of an International Economy* (1940; reprint, Toronto: University of Toronto Press, 1954).

7. William Christian, ed., *The Idea File of Harold Adams Innis,* by Harold A. Innis (Toronto: University of Toronto Press, 1980), xiii.

8. Harold A. Innis, "A History of Communications: An Incomplete and Unrevised Manuscript" (McLennan Library, Montreal; Montreal: McGill University, n.d.), Chapter V, 42, microfiche.

9. Innis, "History of Communications," Chapter V, 43.

10. Innis, "History of Communications," Chapter VI, 81–85.

11. Innis, "History of Communications," Chapter VI, 12.

12. Poem by Richard Frame, printed in Philadelphia in 1692 by William Bradford and cited in Innis, "History of Communications," Chapter VII, 97.

13. Innis, "History of Communications," Chapter VII, 26.

14. Innis, "History of Communications," Chapter VI, 41–44.

15. Innis, "History of Communications," Chapter VI, 67.

16. Tom Cooper, "The Unknown Innis," *Journal of Canadian Studies* 12, no. 5 (Winter 1977): 114–117.

Appendix B

The Contributions of Mary Quayle Innis

J. David Black

Both of us can move mountains.

—Harold A. Innis, in a letter to his fiancée, Mary Quayle, 1919

Mary Quayle Innis is remembered in the Innis scholarship the way a distant relative might be captured in an old family photograph. Her image is demure, understated, and rather formal, someone who typed her husband's manuscripts and stoically raised the couple's four children.

That image is reflected in the scant attention Mary receives in the extensive secondary literature on Innis. Donald Grant Creighton's 1957 biography devotes its only significant statement about the young Mary Quayle to her appearance. A reference to her in the most comprehensive survey of Harold's career identifies her (inaccurately) as a "published poet and arts patron," and their marriage as one with an "extremely conventional gender split" in which Mary served as "keeper of their cultural life."[1] The only Innis scholar to speak of Mary's substance is Irene Spry, who knew her personally and represents her as Harold's "charming and brilliant wife" and a "noted author."[2] Beyond these remarks on Mary's appearance, her belles lettres, and intelligence, the dozens of books and articles on Harold tell us little of the woman to whom he was married for thirty-one years.

The case to be made for better understanding her is more than a matter of feminist scruple—of bringing into focus the woman behind the celebrated man. The more we learn about her life and work, the more room there is for speculation about her influence on Harold's writing. Features of Harold's books that are puzzling in light of his own background may well be explained by Mary's presence.

Mary Quayle was born to a Methodist family on April 13, 1899, in St.

Mary's, Ohio. Her mother, Effie Lloyd, had the opportunity to pursue a course at business college, rare for a woman of the time. Her father, Frederick Quayle, was a British-born tradesman who earned a good living installing telephone systems across the United States. The Quayles traveled regularly until Mary entered high school in Winnetka, Illinois, and her bookishness was tempered with exploration of the dusty towns in which her father was employed.

In unpublished memoirs written not long before her death, she describes

Mary Quayle Innis

scenes of early twentieth-century America like so many slides in a magic lantern show: a wide-eyed visit to a country fair flea circus; an encounter with child laborers and a chain gang in the Deep South; and a terrifying experience of ball lightning as it rolled through the Quayles' rented house. As the following passage from the memoir suggests, Mary remembered her precocious younger self, "I was the girl, the oldest, I brought home only top marks from school, I taught the infant class at Sunday school, was always ready to speak a piece in public, adorned Christmas and birthdays with profusions of embroidery and crochet work, was healthy in the main, loved reading and all such virtuous activities."[3]

Her love of reading and the writing talent that won her several high school writing awards inspired Mary to begin an undergraduate degree in English literature at the University of Chicago in 1915. Founded in 1890 with a major donation from oil magnate John D. Rockefeller, the university was unique for admitting women and minorities at a time when many others did not. At Chicago, Mary also took a number of courses in political economy and history. She left briefly to do war service in Washington, D.C., and returned to finish her degree in the fall of 1918.

In the winter of 1919, she enrolled in a political economy class taught by a young Canadian doctoral student and Great War veteran, Harold A. Innis. It was Harold's first course, and Mary made an impression on the novice instructor. Creighton describes their early acquaintance at Chicago, a campus not known for its romantic atmosphere:

He began to notice her. He found that in her case he could perform the lecturer's duty of fitting a name to a face with surprising ease. Her eyes were wide-set and blue and serious. There was a pensive loveliness in her features and a dignity and elegance in her slight figure. They talked. They went to movies together. She had read a lot, in literary regions where he had not ventured very far. Her intellectual interests were comparable with his, and the quiet determination with which she pursued them equalled his own. By the time spring came he began to realize that he was in love.[4]

Mary and Harold were engaged in the spring of 1920. He submitted his thesis at Chicago in the summer of that year and joined the Department of Political Economy at the University of Toronto in the fall. They were married in Chicago in May 1921, and Mary returned with Harold to his modest apartment in Toronto. The young American found herself living in a country she might have known only as the snowy backdrop in silent films featuring heroic Canadian Mounties.

The marriage confirmed a working relationship that had emerged during their courtship. Mary had accompanied Harold on his doctoral research, visiting libraries, typing manuscripts, and working alongside him as he prepared his dissertation on the Canadian Pacific Railway. After their marriage, Mary joined Harold on research trips relating to the fur trade manuscript, traveling in Europe and across Canada in 1922–1923. Only in 1924, with the birth of the first of their four children, Donald, did Mary stop long enough to assume the role of mother. Three other children would follow—Mary in 1927, Hugh in 1930, and Anne in 1933.

Characteristically, Mary wrote and published short stories during these years of intensive parenting, and the stories would serve later as the basis for her 1943 novel *Stand on a Rainbow*.[5] The novel is an uncomplicated account of a year in the life of a middle-class family, drawn almost entirely from Mary's maternal experience. Because it is so autobiographical, the novel's montage of domestic scenes is revealing in its emotional honesty. Among the trips with the children to the cottage or the park, or during a rainy day at home, there lie hints of the hardship of raising four children while Harold spent long hours at the university building his career.

The Innis daughters, Mary Cates and Anne Innis Dagg, spoke of the marriage's several sides in separate interviews. Cates depicts her parents as having "lived parallel lives, both involved in reading and writing."[6] Dagg describes Mary as being "annoyed" at being taken for a faculty wife, when she thought of herself as a writer and scholar.[7] In their newly built house in north Toronto, which doubled as an intellectual salon and day care, the Innises decided on their only formal research collaboration: *An Economic History of Canada*.[8]

"When you think of how many professors could go home and tell their wife to write a book in their subject, it's amazing," states Dagg.[9] The book was commissioned by Harold as a textbook for a course he taught in Canadian economic history, since no such book existed. Mary, with four children under the age of ten, researched and wrote it with Harold's assistance. The book is a masterpiece of compression and sold well for twenty years. Technical analyses of agriculture and trade are paired with indignant commentary at the "evil conditions" of nineteenth-century industry in which "no laws protected employees from accident, long hours, bad conditions, or child labour."[10]

But her *Economic History of Canada* is more remarkable for what may be the earliest evidence of an Innis writing about communications. Creighton dates Harold's scholarly interest in communications to his 1942 article "The Newspaper in Economic Development," an outgrowth of Innis's curiosity about the pulp and paper industry, among other economic staples in Canadian history.[11] Yet, in *Economic History of Canada,* a text that would be the standard general economic history in Canadian universities for a generation, communication media make more than a cameo appearance.

Postal services, telegraphy, and newspapers feature in the book regularly as means to accelerate economic growth, and there are some twenty-three references to media cited in the index. And, in a manner that foreshadows Harold's "bias of communication" concept, Mary explores the subtle interaction between media and culture. Writing of 1870s' Canada, she argues that "with the improvement of postal facilities came the spread of education, the rise of the newspaper, and the correlated rise of advertising."[12] The conceptual basis for this concatenation of factors is implicit, but the same could be said of Innis's own elliptical writings. It is clear that almost a decade before Harold first made the transition from political economy to communication, Mary had committed ideas about communication to print.

The 1940s elevated Harold to the position of senior academic statesman, and Mary increasingly played hostess to graduate students, faculty, and dignitaries. After some early political battles, Harold's rise was rapid: He became head of political economy at the University of Toronto in 1937; president of the Royal Society of Canada in 1946; and finally dean of graduate studies at the university in 1947. He also began to publish the essays later collected in his three books on communications. Mary kept pace in editing and writing and published a series of historical articles in the *Dalhousie Review* in the late 1930s. After a decade of editing the newsletter of the Young Women's Christian Association (YWCA), she published a history of the YWCA, *Unfold the Years: A History of the Young Women's Christian Association in Canada,* in 1949.[13]

Life was good in Toronto, despite some strain associated with Harold's frequent absences on academic and government business. Mary pored over newspapers, read widely from English literary classics, and listened to weekend classical music concerts on the radio. She researched and wrote a two-volume history of Canada for elementary school students, *Changing Canada,* which appeared in 1951–1952.[14] In Dagg's catalog of women writers of nonfiction in Canada from 1836 to 1945, *The Feminine Gaze: A Canadian Compendium of Non-fiction Women Authors and Their Works, 1836–1945,* she notes that it required "a great deal of ambition for an early woman to write a book and have it published. . . . To write a book of non-fiction indicated that a woman felt her ideas and information should reach a wider audience than the friends and relatives who made up her private sphere."[15]

Then, in July 1950, Harold became seriously ill with the cancer that led to his early death. True to form for the former Baptist farm boy, he alternated hospital stays with his usual rigorous schedule of hard work and travel. Mary was a constant companion during his bouts of illness. Dagg remarks that "when he became sick with cancer, for most of a year she stayed with him, and spent every day at the Western Hospital when he was there."[16] After several brief periods of remission, Harold died at home in 1952, just a few days past his fifty-eighth birthday. Mary was a widow at the age of fifty-three.

With Harold's death, Mary began a second career as a university administrator, participant in government commissions, editor, and writer, a career that paralleled her late husband's. Her first major task was the preparation of new editions of Harold's historical epics, and with S. D. Clark and W. T. Easterbrook assisting, she published *The Cod Fisheries: The History of an International Economy* in 1954 and *The Fur Trade in Canada* in 1956, and edited a collection of Innis's political economy articles, *Essays in Canadian Economic History* in 1956.[17] As "the only one who could read what he had written," Mary decoded Harold's notoriously illegible notes on the previous editions of these volumes and revised the manuscripts in accord with his wishes.[18] It may never be clear just how much revision she did, but her role as Harold's principal editor and her influence on how he is read today have never been fully appreciated. Dagg writes:

> [Mary] Innis updated and improved these books in two ways: by adding references, alone or with notes, that had appeared after the date of publication of the book, and by adding Harold Innis's own questions and comments which had occurred to him since the book was published. These addenda were difficult because of the poor writing and cryptic notations used by Harold Innis which made them difficult to decipher and track down to the source. In all three books she also prepared the indices.[19]

Mary was named dean of women at University College, part of the University of Toronto, in 1955, serving nine years as protector and advisor to thousands of female students. She found an outlet for her social conscience by knitting woollen goods for various causes. She was appointed the only Canadian woman delegate to the Commonwealth Conference on Education in Oxford, England, in 1959, and was made vice chair of the Committee on Religious Education in Ontario public schools after she retired from University College in 1964. She received honorary doctorates from Queen's University in Kingston, Ontario, in 1958, and from the University of Waterloo in Waterloo, Ontario, in 1965. This was overdue recognition of her contributions as a public intellectual to Canadian culture and university life.

During these years, she continued to write and edit. Another volume of history for elementary school students, *Living in Canada,* followed in 1954. She then published a popular account of three journeys into the largely unknown Canadian west in the nineteenth century, *Travellers West;* an edition of the diaries of Lady Simcoe, the talented wife of John Graves Simcoe, the first lieutenant governor of upper Canada; an edited collection of biographical reflections on twenty prominent Canadian women, *The Clear Spirit: Twenty Canadian Women and Their Times;* and an edited series of papers on issues in nursing education, *Nursing Education in a Changing Society.* She also published nonfiction articles in the *United Church Observer,* a publication of the United Church of Canada. Her last work as an editor, a revised edition of Harold's first communications text, *Empire and Communications,* was perhaps her best known. It was published the day after she died suddenly of a stroke on January 10, 1972, at the age of seventy-two.[20]

Perhaps the best evidence of Mary's influence on Harold's work is her life, given the egalitarian intellectual role she played in their marriage. There is the early instance of active assistance with his dissertation, her remarkable references to communications in *Economic History of Canada,* and a lifelong interest in history that was comparable to Harold's. Moreover, their reading habits complemented each other, since Harold read history and social science literature, and Mary read literature and biography.

Dagg speculates that many of the unconventional references to literature, biography, and memoirs in Harold's works come from her mother. "Nobody's ever mentioned this from all the literature on Harold Innis. . . . It's something that struck me as very, very odd in that so many of the sources—if you look at the footnotes in the later work—are memoirs, biographies, and autobiographies. They're not the hard-headed texts of sociologists, historians, and economists. That would have come from my mother, I imagine."[21] Finally, there is the deep familiarity with Harold's work that enabled Mary, a professional writer and editor, to edit four of his texts in both political economy and communications.

Still, there is no apparent formal evidence of collaboration, and the Innis daughters are divided with respect to Mary's influence.[22] For now, barring some yet undiscovered piece of evidence, the most that can be said with certainty is that theirs was a far more complex marriage than the Innis scholarship has observed to date. An unsmiling presence in a faded photograph she was not.

NOTES

1. Charles R. Acland, "Histories of Place and Power," in *Harold Innis in the New Century: Reflections and Refractions,* ed. Charles R. Acland and William J. Buxton (Montreal: McGill-Queen's University Press, 1999), 246. Mary published a small chapbook of poetry while an undergraduate at the University of Chicago. Subsequently, her published creative output consisted of both prose fiction and nonfiction exclusively. And while she may have informally patronized the arts, there is little evidence of extensive membership on boards or significant philanthropy in the literary, dance, or theater worlds. Anne Innis Dagg reports that her mother did serve with the Heliconian Club, a Toronto-based club for women interested in arts and letters.

2. Irene Spry, "Economic History and Economic Theory," in *Harold Innis in the New Century: Reflections and Refractions,* ed. Charles R. Acland and William J. Buxton (Montreal: McGill-Queen's University Press, 1999), 108. Barbara Pell's entry on Mary in the "Cana-

dian Writers Series" of the *Dictionary of Literary Biography* (vol. 88, Detroit, Mich.: Gale Research, 1989) was very helpful as a source of information about Mary and is the only piece of writing apart from Dagg's own to address Mary as an intellectual and writer. Pell is a professor in the religion, culture, and ethics program at British Columbia's Trinity Western University.

3. Mary Quayle Innis, unfinished memoir, file 13, Mary Quayle Innis Collection, GA127, University of Waterloo Archives, 47–48.

4. Donald Grant Creighton, *Harold Adams Innis: Portrait of a Scholar* (1957; reprint, Toronto: University of Toronto Press, 1978), 42.

5. Mary Quayle Innis, *Stand on a Rainbow* (Toronto: Collins, 1943).

6. Mary Cates, e-mail to the author, September 1, 2002.

7. Anne Innis Dagg, interview by the author, Waterloo, Ontario, August 15, 2002.

8. Mary Quayle Innis, *An Economic History of Canada* (Toronto: Ryerson, 1935).

9. Dagg, interview. Dagg has written elsewhere that her mother "felt frustrated as a serious writer and academic, the areas of greatest importance to her, probably because of the way she felt marginalized by others," who saw her only as Harold's wife and the mother of his children. See Anne Innis Dagg, "Mary Quayle Innis As Economic Historian," file 1, Mary Quayle Innis Collection, GA127, University of Waterloo Archives, 8. This manuscript was published as an encyclopedia entry for Mary in Mary Ann Dimand, Robert W. Dimand, and Evelyn L. Forget, eds., *Women of Value: Feminist Essays on the History of Women in Economics* (Aldershot, UK: Edward Elgar, 1995).

10. Innis, *Economic History of Canada,* 212.

11. Harold A. Innis, "The Newspaper in Economic Development," *Journal of Economic History* 2/s (1942): 1–33.

12. Innis, *Economic History of Canada,* 191.

13. Mary Quayle Innis, *Unfold the Years: A History of the Young Women's Christian Association in Canada* (Toronto: McClelland and Stewart, 1949).

14. Mary Quayle Innis, *Changing Canada,* 2 vols. (Toronto: Clarke, Irwin, 1951–1952).

15. Anne Innis Dagg, *The Feminine Gaze: A Canadian Compendium of Non-fiction Women Authors and Their Works, 1836–1945* (Waterloo: Wilfrid Laurier University Press, 2001), 13. All four children in turn entered and graduated from the University of Toronto between 1943 and 1956. After doctoral work in biology, Dagg became an advisor in the independent studies program at the University of Waterloo. She has published a number of books in zoology, feminism, and Canadian history. Cates married a surgeon, raised a family in British Columbia, and did graduate work in French literature. She now resides in San Diego, California. Hugh is a professor in the School of Image Arts at Ryerson University in Toronto, appears as a frequent political commentator on radio and television, and continues to feature as a keynote speaker at a number of events. The oldest brother, Donald, became a geography professor at the State University of New York, Geneseo. Donald died in 1988.

16. Dagg, interview.

17. Mary Quayle Innis with S. D. Clarke and W. T. Easterbrook, eds., *The Cod Fisheries: The History of an International Economy,* by Harold A. Innis, rev. ed. (Toronto: University of Toronto Press, 1954); Mary Quayle Innis with S. D. Clarke and W. T. Easterbrook, eds., *The Fur Trade in Canada,* by Harold A. Innis, rev. ed. (Toronto: University of Toronto Press, 1956); Mary Quayle Innis, ed., *Essays in Canadian Economic History,* by Harold A. Innis (Toronto: University of Toronto Press, 1956).

18. Dagg, interview.

19. Dagg, "Mary Quayle Innis As Economic Historian," 6.

20. Mary Quayle Innis with Alex A. Cameron and Arnold Boggs, *Living in Canada* (Toronto: Clarke, Irwin, 1954); Mary Quayle Innis, *Travelers West* (Toronto: Clarke, Irwin, 1956); Mary Quayle Innis, ed., *Mrs. Simcoe's Diary,* by Elizabeth Simcoe (New York: St. Martin's, 1965); Mary Quayle Innis, ed., *The Clear Spirit: Twenty Canadian Women and Their Times* (Toronto: University of Toronto Press for the Canadian Federation of University Women, 1966); Mary Quayle Innis, ed., *Nursing Education in a Changing Society* (Toronto: University of Toronto Press, 1970); Mary Quayle Innis, ed., *Empire and Communications,* by Harold A. Innis, rev. ed. (Toronto: University of Toronto Press, 1972).

21. Dagg, interview.

22. Cates stated in a September 1, 2002, e-mail that she did "not believe there was any influence of one upon the other. My mother was a very remarkable woman, who had a very interesting life, and I think she can be respected on those terms."

A Select Bibliography

The following list is intended as a student's guide to the major publications of Harold A. Innis. Many, but by no means all, of his voluminous output of journal articles can be found in the anthologies cited in this bibliography.

PRIMARY SOURCES

Innis, Harold A. *The Bias of Communication*. 1951. Reprint, with an introduction by Paul Heyer and David Crowley, Toronto: University of Toronto Press, 1995.
———. *Changing Concepts of Time*. 1952. Reprint, with a foreword by James W. Carey, Boulder, Colo.: Rowman & Littlefield, 2003.
———. *The Cod Fisheries: The History of an International Economy*. 1940. Reprint, Toronto: University of Toronto Press, 1954.
———. "The Concept of Monopoly and Civilization." (1951). In *Staples, Markets, and Cultural Change: Selected Essays, Harold Innis*, ed. Daniel Drache. Montreal: McGill-Queens University Press, 1995.
———, ed. *The Dairy Industry in Canada*. Toronto: Ryerson, 1937.
———, ed. *The Diary of Alexander James McPhail*. Toronto: University of Toronto Press, 1940.
———, et al. *The Diary of Simeon Perkins*. 5 vols. Westport, Conn.: Greenwood, 1969–1978.
———. *Empire and Communications*. 1950. Reprint, with a foreword by Marshall McLuhan, Toronto: University of Toronto Press, 1975.
———. *Empire and Communications*. Ed. David Godfrey. Victoria, British Columbia: Porcepic, 1986.
———. "The English Press in the Nineteenth Century: An Economic Approach." *University of Toronto Quarterly* 15 (1945): 37–53.
———. *Essays in Canadian Economic History*. Ed. Mary Q. Innis. Toronto: University of Toronto Press, 1962.
———. *The Fur Trade in Canada*. 1930. Reprint, New Haven, Conn.: Yale University Press, 1962.

————. *A History of the Canadian Pacific Railway*. 1923. Reprint, Toronto: University of Toronto Press, 1971.

————. "A History of Communications: An Incomplete and Unrevised Manuscript." McLennan Library, Montreal. Montreal: McGill University, n.d.

————. *The Idea File of Harold Adams Innis*. Ed. William Christian. Toronto: University of Toronto Press, 1980.

————. *Innis on Russia: The Russian Diary and Other Writings*. Ed. William Christian. Toronto: The Harold Innis Foundation, 1981.

————. "The Newspaper in Economic Development." *Journal of Economic History* 2/s (1942): 1–33.

————, ed. *Peter Pond: Fur Trader and Adventurer*. Toronto: Irwin and Gordon, 1930.

————. *Political Economy and the Modern State*. Toronto: University of Toronto Press, 1946.

————, ed. *Select Documents in Canadian Economic History*. Toronto: University of Toronto Press, 1929.

————. *The Strategy of Culture*. Toronto: University of Toronto Press, 1952.

SECONDARY SOURCES

Acland, Charles R., and William J. Buxton, eds. *Harold Innis in the New Century: Reflections and Refractions*. Montreal: McGill-Queen's University Press, 1995.

Ascher, Robert, and Marcia Ascher. *Code of the Quipu: A Study in Media, Mathematics, and Culture*. Ann Arbor, Mich.: University of Michigan Press, 1981.

Babe, Robert E. *Canadian Communication Thought: Ten Foundational Writers*. Toronto: University of Toronto Press, 2000.

Berton, Pierre. *The National Dream: The Great Railway, 1871–1881*. Toronto: McClelland and Stewart, 1970.

Braudel, Fernand. *La Méditerranée at le monde méditerranée à l'époque de Philippe II*. Paris: Librairie Armand Colin, 1949.

Bücher, Karl. *Industrial Evolution*. Trans. Samuel Morley Wickett. New York: Henry Holt, 1901.

Buxton, William J. "The Bias against Communication: On the Neglect and Non-publication of the 'Incomplete and Unrevised Manuscript' of Harold Adams Inns." *Canadian Journal of Communication* 26, nos. 2–3 (2001).

Carey, James W. *Communication As Culture: Essays on Media and Society*. Boston: Unwin Hyman, 1989.

————. "Harold Adams Innis and Marshall McLuhan." *The Antioch Review* 27, no. 1 (Spring 1967).

Carpenter, Edmund, and Marshall McLuhan, eds. *Explorations in Communication*. Boston: Beacon: 1960.

Childe, Gordon. *Man Makes Himself*. London: Watts, 1936.

————. *What Happened in History*. Harmondsworth, UK: Penguin, 1942.

Christian, William, ed. *The Idea File of Harold Adams Innis*, by Harold A. Innis. Toronto: University of Toronto Press, 1980.

Cochrane, Charles Norris. *Christianity and Classical Culture: A Study of Thought and Action from Augustus to Augustine*. London: Oxford University Press, 1944.

Coe Michael D. *The Maya*. London: Thames and Hudson, 1987.

Cohen, Hart. "Margins at the Centre: Innis' Concept of Bias to the Development of Aboriginal Media." *Continuum: The Australian Journal of Media and Culture* 7, no. 1 (1993): 105–120.

Cooper, Tom. "The Unknown Innis." *Journal of Canadian Studies* 12, no. 5 (Winter 1977): 114–117.

Creighton, Donald Grant. *Harold Adams Innis: Portrait of a Scholar*. 1957. Reprint, Toronto: University of Toronto Press, 1978.

Crowley, David, and Paul Heyer. *Communication in History: Technology, Culture, Society*. Boston: Allyn and Bacon, 2003.

Crowley, David, and David Mitchell, eds. *Communication Theory Today*. Stanford, Calif.: Stanford University Press, 1994.

Czitrom, Daniel J. *Media and the American Mind: From Morse to McLuhan*. Chapel Hill: University of North Carolina Press, 1982.

Dagg, Anne Innis. *The Feminine Gaze: A Canadian Compendium of Non-fiction Women Authors and Their Works, 1836–1945*. Waterloo: Wilfrid Laurier University Press, 2001.

———. "Mary Quayle Innis As an Economic Historian." In *Women of Value: Feminist Essays in the History of Women in Economics*, ed. Mary Ann Dimand, Robert W. Dimand, and Evelyn L. Forget. Aldershot, UK: Edward Elgar, 1995.

Deibert, Ronald. *Parchment, Printing, and Hypermedia: Communication in World Order Transformation*. New York: Columbia University Press, 1997.

Derrida, Jacques. *Of Grammatology*. Trans. Gayatri Chakravorty Spivak. Baltimore, Md.: Johns Hopkins University Press, 1976.

Diamond, Stanley. *The Search for the Primitive: A Critique of Civilization*. New Brunswick, N.J.: Transaction, 1994.

Dimand, Mary Ann, Robert W. Dimand, and Evelyn L. Forget, eds. *Women of Value: Feminist Essays on the History of Women in Economics*. Aldershot, UK: Edward Elgar, 1995.

Drache, Daniel, ed. *Staples, Markets, and Cultural Change: Harold Innis*. Montreal: McGill-Queen's University Press, 1995.

Drucker, Johanna. *The Alphabetic Labyrinth: Letters in History and Imagination*. London: Thames and Hudson, 1995.

Duncan, David Ewing. *Calendar*. New York: Avon, 1998.

Eco, Umberto. *The Name of the Rose*. Trans. William Weaver. San Diego: Harcourt Brace Jovanovich, 1983.

———. *The Name of the Rose*. Dir. Jean-Jacques Annaud. 20th Century Fox Film Corporation, 1986.

Ellul, Jacques. *The Technological Society*. New York: Knopf, 1964.

Engels, Friedrich. *The Origin of the Family, Private Property, and the State*. 1884. Reprint, Chicago: Kerr, 1902.

George, Peter. Foreword to *A History of the Canadian Pacific Railway*, by Harold A. Innis. 1923. Reprint, Toronto: University of Toronto Press, 1971.

Giedion, Sigfried. *Mechanization Takes Command: A Contribution to Anonymous History*. New York: Oxford University Press, 1948.

Goldberg, Bernard. *Bias: A CBS Insider Exposes How the Media Distorts the News*. Washington, D.C.: Regency, 2001.

Goody, Jack. *The Domestication of the Savage Mind*. Cambridge: Cambridge University Press, 1977.

————. *Literacy in Traditional Societies.* Cambridge: Cambridge University Press, 1968.

————. *The Logic of Writing and the Organization of Society.* Cambridge: Cambridge University Press, 1986.

Hardt, Hanno. *Social Theories of the Press.* Boulder, Colo.: Rowman & Littlefield, 2001.

Harold Innis: Patterns in Communication. Prod. and dir. Alison Beale. 52 min. 1990. Videocassette.

Havelock, Eric. *Harold A. Innis: A Memoir.* Toronto: The Harold Innis Foundation, 1982.

Hegel, Georg. *Philosophy of History.* Trans. John Sibree. 1899. Reprint, preface by Charles Hegel and introduction by C. J. Friedrich, New York: Dover, 1956.

Heyer, Paul. *Communications and History: Theories of Media, Knowledge, and Civilization.* Westport, Conn.: Greenwood, 1988.

————. "Empire, History, and Communications Viewed from the Margins: The Legacies of Gordon Childe and Harold Innis." *Continuum: The Australian Journal of Media and Culture* 7, no. 1 (1993): 91–104.

Houseman, John. *Entertainers and the Entertained.* New York: Simon and Schuster, 1986.

Innis, Mary Quayle. *Changing Canada.* 2 vols. Toronto: Clarke, Irwin, 1951–1952.

————, ed. *The Clear Spirit: Twenty Canadian Women and Their Times.* Toronto: University of Toronto Press for the Canadian Federation of University Women, 1966.

————. *An Economic History of Canada.* Toronto: Ryerson, 1935.

————, ed. *Empire and Communications,* by Harold A. Innis. Rev. ed. Toronto: University of Toronto Press, 1972.

————, ed. *Essays in Canadian Economic History,* by Harold A. Innis. Toronto: University of Toronto Press, 1956.

————, ed. *Mrs. Simcoe's Diary,* by Elizabeth Simcoe. New York: St. Martin's, 1965.

————, ed. *Nursing Education in a Changing Society.* Toronto: University of Toronto Press, 1970.

————. *Stand on a Rainbow.* Toronto: Collins, 1943.

————. *Travelers West.* Toronto: Clarke, Irwin, 1956.

————. *Unfold the Years: A History of the Young Women's Christian Association in Canada.* Toronto: McClelland and Stewart, 1949.

Innis, Mary Quayle, with Alex A. Cameron and Arnold Boggs. *Living in Canada.* Toronto: Clarke, Irwin, 1954.

Innis, Mary Quayle, with S. D. Clarke and W. T. Easterbrook, eds. *The Cod Fisheries: The History of an International Economy,* by Harold A. Innis. Rev. ed. Toronto: University of Toronto Press, 1954.

————, eds. *The Fur Trade in Canada,* by Harold A. Innis. Rev. ed. Toronto: University of Toronto Press, 1956.

Kerckhove, Derrick de. "McLuhan and the Toronto School of Communication." *Canadian Journal of Communication* 14, nos. 4–5 (December 1989): 73–79.

Kroeber, Alfred. *Configurations of Culture Growth.* Berkeley: University of California Press, 1944.

Kroker, Arthur. *Technology and the Canadian Mind: Innis, McLuhan, Grant.* Montreal: New World Perspectives, 1984.

Kroker, Arthur, and Marilouise Kroker. *Ideology and Power in the Age of Lenin in Ruins.* New York: St. Martin's, 1991.

————, eds. *The Panic Encyclopedia: The Definitive Guide to the Postmodern Scene.* Montreal: New World Perspectives, 1989.

Kuhns, William. *The Post-industrial Prophets: Interpretations of Technology*. New York: Weybright and Talley, 1971.

Maine, Henry Sumner. *Ancient Law: Its Connection with the Early History of Society, and Its Relation to Modern Ideas*. London: Murray, 1866.

Marx, Karl. *Capital*. Vol. 1. 1867. Reprint, New York: International, 1972.

―――. *A Contribution to the Critique of Political Economy*. Trans. Nahum I. Stone. 1859. Reprint. New York: International, 1970.

―――. *The Ethnological Notebooks of Karl Marx*. Ed. and trans. Lawrence Krader. Assen, The Netherlands: Van Gorcum, 1972.

Marx, Karl, and Friedrich Engels. *The German Ideology*. New York: International, 1972.

McLuhan, Marshall. Foreword to *Empire and Communications*, by Harold A. Innis. 1950; reprint, Toronto: University of Toronto Press, 1975.

―――. *The Gutenberg Galaxy: The Making of a Typographic Man*. New York: Signet, 1969.

―――. *The Mechanical Bride: Folklore of Industrial Man*. Boston: Beacon, 1967.

―――. Foreword to *The Bias of Communication*, by Harold A. Innis. Toronto: University of Toronto Press, 1964.

―――. *Understanding Media: The Extensions of Man*. New York: Signet, 1964.

Melody, William, Liora Salter, and Paul Heyer, eds. *Culture, Communication, and Dependency: The Tradition of H. A. Innis*. Norwood, N.J.: Ablex, 1981.

Meyrowitz, Joshua. *No Sense of Place: The Impact of Electronic Media on Social Behavior*. New York: Oxford University Press, 1986.

Molinaro, Matie, Corinne McLuhan, and William Toye, eds. *The Letters of Marshall McLuhan*. New York: Oxford University Press, 1987.

Morgan, Lewis Henry. *League of the Ho-de-no-sau-nee or Iroquois*. New York: Franklin, 1862.

Mumford, Lewis. *Technics and Civilization*. New York: Harcourt, Brace, 1934.

Neill, Robin. *A New Theory of Value: The Canadian Economics of H. A. Innis*. Toronto: University of Toronto Press, 1972.

Parkman, Francis. *Francis Parkman's Works*. Toronto: Morceny, 1900.

Patterson, Graeme. *History and Communications: Harold Innis, Marshall McLuhan, and the Interpretation of History*. Toronto: University of Toronto Press, 1990.

Postman, Neil. *Amusing Ourselves to Death*. New York: Penguin, 1986.

―――. *Building a Bridge to the Eighteenth Century: How the Past Can Improve Our Future*. New York: Knopf, 1999.

―――. *The Disappearance of Childhood*. New York: Laurel, 1984.

―――. *Technopoly: The Surrender of Culture to Technology*. New York: Knopf, 1992.

Radin, Paul. *Primitive Man As Philosopher*. New York: Appleton, 1927.

Rosenthal, Raymond, ed. *McLuhan Pro and Con*. Baltimore, Md.: Penguin, 1969.

Rousseau, Jean Jacques, and Johann Gottfried Herder. *On the Origin of Language*. New York: Unger, 1966.

Rousseau, Jean-Jacques. "The Discourse on the Origin and Foundation of Inequality among Men." In *Jean-Jacques Rousseau: The First and Second Discourses*, ed. Roger D. Masters. New York: St. Martin's, 1964.

Sapir, Edward. "Culture, Genuine, and Spurious." *American Journal of Sociology* 29 (1924).

Shoesmith, Brian. "Introduction to Innis' 'History of Communication.'" *Continuum: The Australian Journal of Media and Culture* 7, no. 1 (1993): 121–131.

Smith, Adam. *Inquiry into the Nature and Causes of the Wealth of Nations*. 1776; reprint, Buffalo, N.Y.: Prometheus, 1991.

————. *The Theory of Moral Sentiments*. 1759. Reprint, Amherst, N.Y.: Prometheus, 2000.

Stocking, George W. *Race, Culture, and Evolution: Essays in the History of Anthropology*. New York: The Free Press, 1968.

Theall, Donald. *The Virtual McLuhan*. Montreal: McGill-Queen's University Press, 2001.

Tylor, Edward Burnet. *Researches into the Early History of Mankind and the Development of Civilization*. Chicago: University of Chicago Press, 1864.

Veblen, Thorstein. *Theory of Business Enterprise*. New York: Scribner's, 1904.

————. *Theory of the Leisure Class: An Economic Study in the Evolution of Institutions*. New York: Macmillan, 1899.

Wallas, Graham. *Social Judgment*. London: Allen and Unwin, 1934.

Watson, John. "Harold Innis and Classical Scholarship." *Journal of Canadian Studies* 12, no. 5 (1977).

Wright, Ronald. *Stolen Continents: The Americas through Indian Eyes since 1492*. Boston: Houghton Mifflin, 1992.

Index

advertising, 78–89
alphabet, 69, 70
American cultural influence on Canada, 78–79
American Mercury (periodical), 78
Amusing Ourselves to Death, Technopoly: The Surrender of Culture to Technology (Postman), 93
Ancient Law (Maine), 50
Annales (periodical), 105
Ascher, Marcia and Robert, 68

Babe, Robert E., 98
Becker, Carl, 47
Berton, Pierre, 6
Beverly Hillbillies, The, 88
Bias of Communication (Innis), 4, 31, 34, 38, 39, 41, 46, 53, 55, 60, 61, 62, 64, 65, 79, 85, 86, 88, 90, 106, 107
Block, Marc, 105
Braudel, Fernand, 105
Broeke, James Ten, 61
Bücher, Karl, 55
Building a Bridge to the Eighteenth Century: How the Past Can Improve the Future (Postman), 93

Cabot, John, 23
Canadian Communication Thought: Ten Foundational Writers (Babe), 98
Canadian Journal of Economics and Political Science, 42

Capital (Marx), 70
Carey, James W., 4, 86, 89, 90, 91, 92, 93, 96, 101
Carpenter, Edmund, 87, 88, 94
Castor canadensis, 11
Cates, Mary, 116
Changing Canada (Quayle), 117
Changing Concepts of Time (Innis), 34, 55, 62, 90, 95, 78, 79
Childe, Gordon, 47, 52–53, 65, 77, 102
Christian, William, 106
Christianity and Classical Culture: A Study of Thought and Action from Augustus to Augustine (Cochrane), 41
Citizen Kane, 36
Cochrane, Charles Norris, 41, 42
Code of the Quipu: A Study of Media Mathematics and Culture (Asher and Asher), 68
Cod Fisheries (Innis), 16, 18, 22–24, 34
Cod Fisheries: The History of an International Economy, The (Innis), 13, 30, 105
Communication as Culture: Essays on Media and Society (Carey), 89
communications history, 52
compagnons, 109
Condorcet, Marquis de, 54
Configurations of Culture Growth (Kroeber), 54, 61
Continuum: The Australian Journal of Media and Culture, 96
Contribution to the Critique of Political Economy, A (Marx), 70

129

Creighton, Donald Grant, 113, 115, 116
Czitrom, Daniel J., 92, 102

Dagg, Anne Innis, 87, 116, 117, 118, 119;
mother's influence on Harold's work,
119; speaking of her mother, 116, 117,
118
Daily News, 36
Daily Telegraph, 36
Dalhousie Review, 72, 117
Diamond, Stanley, 69
Diary of Alexander James McPhail, The
(Innis), 21
Diebert, Ronald, 97, 101
Disappearance of Childhood, The (Postman),
93
Domestication of the Savage Mind, The
(Goody), 90
Drache, Daniel, 97

Easterbrook, W. T., 87
Eco, Umberto, 77
Economic History of Canada, An (Innis and
Quayle), 116, 119
Egypt, 47, 66, 76–77
Ellul, Jacques, 80
Empire and Communications (Innis), 31, 34,
42, 43, 45, 46, 52, 53, 54, 55, 64, 68, 71,
76, 86, 90, 104, 105, 107, 109, 110, 119
Engels, Friedrich, 70, 71
Erasmus, 110
Explorations (periodical), 87, 88, 90, 91

Febre, Lucien, 105
*Feminine Gaze: A Canadian Compendium of
Non-fiction Women Authors and Their
Works, 1838–1945, The* (Dagg), 117
Foucault, Michel, 101, 102
Freud, Sigmund, 38
fur trade, 11–13; and corporate rivalries,
12–13; in relation to fish and lumber, 13
Fur Trader in Canada, The (Innis), 7, 11–12,
13, 16, 22, 71, 105

Gadus morhua, 23
Giedion, Sigfried, 80

Goffman, Erving, 94
Goody, Jack, 90, 94
Grant, George, 94
Greece, 66, 70, 71, 77, 80, 82; and oral tra-
dition, 66
*Gutenberg Galaxy: The Making of Typographic
Man, The* (McLuhan), 67, 86, 93

*Harold Innis in the New Century: Reflections
and Refractions*, 97
Harold Innis: Patterns in Communication, 96
Havelock, Eric, 31–32, 41, 42, 69, 90, 94
Hearst, William Randolph, 36, 77
Hegel, George, 42–43, 44, 61
Herodotus, 79
Histories (Herodotus), 79
*History of Communications: An Incomplete and
Unrevised Manuscript* (Innis), 103–111;
synopsis of, 106–108
*History and Communications: Harold Innis,
Marshall McLuhan, and the Interpretation of
History* (Patterson), 96
History of the Canadian Pacific Railway, A
(Innis), 3, 5–6; synopsis of, 5–6
Hitler, Adolf, 46
Homer, 66
Houseman, John, 88

Idea File of Harold Adams Innis (Innis), 41, 60
Iliad, The (Homer), 66
Incas, 68
Industrial Evolution (Bücher), 55
Innis, Harold Adams: beginnings as a
teacher, 5; bout with cancer and death,
85; compared to Gordon Childe, 53–54;
critiqued by James Carey, 89; critique of
education, 81–83; education of, 2, 3, 4,
5; enlisting in the Great War, 3, 4; family
history, 1–2; interest in the railway, 3,
5–6, 7, 46; marriage to Mary Quayle, 5;
and monopoly of knowledge, 76, 77, 78;
and political economy, 5, 8; post-mor-
tem publications of and by, 94–98; in
relation to George Herbert Mead and
Robert Ezra Park, 4; in relation to Marshall McLuhan, 85–97, 89, 91, 92; in

relation to Neil Postman, 93; and the
Royal Commission of Transportation,
45; staples research, 46; work in acade-
mia, 14, 20, 42; writing on radio, 20

Jonson, Ben, 110
Journal of Economic History, 30

Kerchkove, Derrick de, 90
Kroeber, Alfred, 54, 61, 105
Kroker, Arthur, 94–96

literacy, 67, 77
Literacy in Traditional Societies (Goody), 90
Living in Canada (Quayle), 118
Logan, Robert, 90
Logic of Writing and the Organization of Society
(Goody), 90
Long, John, 8
lumber trades, 21. *See also* staples research

Maine, Henry Summer, 50
Man Make Himself (Childe), 53
Marx, Karl, 25, 38, 39, 45, 70, 76
Mayan civilization, 65
McLuhan, Marshall, 4, 31, 42, 44, 46, 55,
59, 60, 61, 62, 70, 85–96, 97, 98, 101,
102; in relation to Innis, 85–87, 89, 91,
92
Mead, George Herbert, 4, 45
*Mechanical Bride: Folklore of Industrial Man,
The* (McLuhan), 85, 87, 93
*Media and the American Mind: From Morse to
McLuhan* (Czitrom), 92
medium theory, 94
Mein Kampf (Hitler), 46
Mencken, H. L., 78
Meyrowitz, Joshua, 92, 93–94, 101
"Minerva's Owl," 42, 61; and Greek liter-
acy, 44
Mirror (Hearst), 37
Mission to Moscow (film), 33
monopoly of knowledge, 51, 53, 62, 68,
76–78, 81, 89, 98, 102, 106; and oral
cultures, 76; and writing, 76–77
Moret, Alexander, 47

Morgan, Lewis Henry, 71
Mumford, Lewis, 64, 80

Name of the Rose, The (Eco, film and novel),
77
*National Dream: The Great Railway, 1871–
1881, The* (Innis), 6
Neill, Robin, 103
newspapers, 36; and advertising, 36–37
New York Sun, 36
*No Sense of Place: The Impact of Electronic
Media on Social Behaviour* (Meyrowitz),
93, 94

Odyssey (Homer), 66
Ong, Walter, 90, 94
oral tradition, 47, 49, 50, 61, 64, 66, 68, 69,
70, 71, 89, 98; and Greece, 66
*Origin of the Family, Private Property and the
State, The* (Engels), 71
Otterville, Ontario, 2
Owen, Edward Thomas, 41, 42

paper, 51; history of, 51; and literacy, 51
Paper Chase, The (film), 88
papyrus, 65, 66; influence on written com-
munication, 66; in relation to space-bias,
65
*Parchment, Printing, and Hypermedia: Commu-
nication in World Order Transformation*
(Diebert), 97
Park, Robert Ezra, 4, 55, 86
Parkman, Francis, 70
Patterson, Graeme, 96
Perkins, Simeon, 24
Peter Pond: Fur Trader and Adventurer (Innis),
13
Philosophy of History (Hegel), 42
Playhouse (television program), 90
political economy, 26, 33, 35, 38, 43, 60, 63
Political Economy in the Modern State (Innis),
34–35, 37, 38, 44, 105, 106
Pond, Peter, 14
*Post-industrial Prophets: Interpretations of Tech-
nology* (Kuhns), 91
Postman, Neil, 92, 93

Primitive Man as Philosopher (Radin), 71
print, 67, 80, 81
Pullitzer, Joseph, 36

Quayle, Mary, 5, 15, 113–119; childbirth
    of, 116; death, 119; education, 115; fam-
    ily history, 113–114; influence on Haro-
    ld's work, 118–119; life after Harold,
    117–118; life in Toronto, 117; marriage
    to Harold, 115; as a student of Harold,
    115; work in academia, 117–118

Radin, Paul, 71
*Researches in the Early History of Mankind and
    the Development of Civilization* (Tylor), 54
Rousseau, Jean-Jacques, 54, 69–70

Sapir, Edward, 71–72
Select Documents in Canadian Economic History
    (Innis), 11
Social Judgment (Wallas), 81
Song of Russia (film), 33
*Southwestern Political and Social Science Quar-
    terly*, 16
space-bias, 15, 46, 51, 62, 64, 65, 66–68,
    71, 89, 98; influence on Greece, 66
Spry, Irene, 113
Stand on a Rainbow (Quayle), 116
Staple of News, The (Jonson), 110
*Staples, Markets, and Cultural Change: Harold
    Innis* (Drache), 97
staples research, 21–22, 26, 30

Technics and Civilization (Mumford), 64, 80
*Technology and the Canadian Mind: Innis,
    McLuhan, Grant* (Kroker), 94, 95

Theory of Business Enterprise (Veblen), 16
*Theory of the Leisure Class: An Economic Study
    in the Evolution of Institutions* (Veblen), 16
time-bias, 15, 46, 50, 51, 62–63, 65–68, 71,
    89, 98; and first civilizations, 63; influ-
    ence on Greece, 66; and social control,
    63–64
Toronto School, 90, 94
Travellers West (Quayle), 118
Turgot, Anne-Robert-Jacques, 54
Tylor, Edward Burnet, 54

Understanding Media: The Extensions of Man
    (McLuhan), 37, 46, 89, 93
*Unfold the Years: A History of the Young Wom-
    en's Christian Association in Canada*
    (Quayle), 117
United Church Observer, 118

Veblen, Thorstein, 16, 25, 44, 45, 50, 75,
    92

Wallas, Graham, 81
Watt, Ian, 90
Weber, Max, 69, 89
Welles, Orson, 36, 88
wheat production, 21. *See also* staples
    research
Wilde, Oscar, 89
Wired, 92
Wright, Chester W., 5
writing, 46–47, 49–50, 76; evolution of,
    47, 48; and literacy, 50; and monopoly
    of knowledge, 76–77; and oral culture,
    49; and papyrus, 47, 48–50; and Phoeni-
    cian alphabet, 49; in relation to social
    formations, 48

About the Author

Paul Heyer is professor of communication studies at Wilfrid Laurier University, Waterloo, Ontario, Canada. He is the author of *Communications and History: Theories of Media, Knowledge, and Civilization*, *TITANIC Legacy: Disaster as Media Event and Myth*, and coeditor (with David Crowley) of the introductory textbook, *Communication in History: Technology, Culture, Society*.